Drugspeak

Drugspeak
The Analysis of Drug Discourse

John Booth Davies
University of Strathclyde, UK

harwood academic publishers
Australia • Canada • China • France • Germany • India
Japan • Luxembourg • Malaysia • The Netherlands
Russia • Singapore • Switzerland • Thailand
United Kingdom

Copyright © 1997 OPA (Overseas Publishers Association) Amsterdam B.V. Published in The Netherlands by Harwood Academic Publishers.

Amsteldijk 166
1st Floor
1079 LH Amsterdam
The Netherlands

British Library Cataloguing in Publication Data

Davies, John Booth
 Drugspeak : the analysis of drug discourse
    1. Drug abuse – Terminology
    I. Title
    362.2'9'014

ISBN 90-5702-192-7 (Softcover)

Dedication

ME ME ME ME ME ME ME ME ME ME ME ME

Let's not pretend I'm one of those wonderful people who write books for somebody else.

CONTENTS

Preface

When I was three years old I had a rabbit called Peter. He died in the middle of a thunderstorm, and everyone said it was a heart attack. They told me he was dead, but I did not fully accept their opinions. When I asked them how they knew he was dead they could only present reasons that, so far as I could see, were entirely circumstantial and depended crucially on definitions of 'dead' that I felt were highly arbitrary. Of course, at the time I could not articulate these misgivings, so I just stood there and said "No he's not". I continued to feed him and take him for walks, though I was forced to acknowledge that he had gone very stiff and was suffering a certain loss of appetite. However, this in my view did not mean he was necessarily dead. I figured, or perhaps hoped, he might be doing it on purpose, that he wasn't so much in the grip of some dreadful state, as exercising his free will in an area I didn't fully understand for reasons that eluded me. He didn't move much, however, and I had to agree that, dead or not, a certain amount of the fun had gone out of the relationship. From a philosophical standpoint, the issue remains unresolved to this day. My family however found its resources severely taxed in devising covert and disguised methodologies for separating small boys from large dead rabbits with a minimum of fuss. This difficulty in accepting the completely obvious has always been one of my main failings.

For reasons which are as much personal as scientific, I find myself either sceptical about, or deeply in disagreement with, much of what is written about the 'addicted' state. The personal reasons are neither deep nor fundamental. They centre around nothing more substantial than an unease about bodies of theory with which nearly everyone appears to agree; and a scientifically unacknowledgable conviction that when everyone agrees about something it must be wrong. At the very least, where the major conceptualisations of a phenomenon appear clear cut and plain for all to see, it is obviously high time for a concerted effort to pull the rug from under it. For example, along with theories of addiction, I also regret the fact that the theory of evolution, which is so obviously reasonable and makes sense of so much biodiversity, has not been the subject of more concerted and determined attempts to undermine it. It's too comfy; it's too rational; and if we are not careful we will be stuck with it for ever. And I just don't like the sound of that.

I am also concerned about certain areas of social science methodology, and about the accumulation of 'scientific' work which piles up in a proliferating mass of journals. It appears to me that only a small proportion of it is likely to have lasting value. I suspect that, all too often, the real motivation is not to advance the cause of science at all, but to preserve or improve the ratings in the next research assessment exercise by whatever means are necessary. I do not think that is an appropriate driving force for genuine discovery or even deep discussion. I have also started to believe that a section of this literature, namely that which makes use of verbal reports of various kinds, might actually be misconceived, and therefore highly misleading as a guide for public policy. I am also intrigued as to why increasingly I find the most insightful and exciting material in novels and newspapers rather than psychology books, and I am thinking of recommending James Kelman's *How Late It Was, How Late It Was* as the new basic text in social psychology.

In a previous book, *The Myth of Addiction*, I expressed some strongly-held views about addiction, and obliquely about psychological studies of this alleged condition. I was quite angry about some of the things I felt were wrong with this particular illness-treatment-research cycle, but I think I managed to keep this under control for large sections of that book, and to appear 'scientific' and disinterested, rather than overly partisan. This time, I think I have not done quite so well, largely because my faith in an objective and disinterested science has been shaken to its foundations in recent times by the writings of a number of philosophers which, I confess to my shame, I have only recently read. As a result, I do not claim the ideas presented here are true, since I am now quite uncertain about what 'truth' is; but perhaps some people will find them challenging or at least worthy of a second glance. I believe that within the academic community there is a legitimate place for the novel (in both senses), the unorthodox, the anarchistic, the revolutionary and the downright scurrilous, without people becoming defensive and tight-lipped because someone is trying to storm their castle. It appears that in some circles, for example, recent writings on the philosophy of science, post modernism, discourse analysis, the social construction of reality, and other topics, are seen as forces to be resisted or even denigrated, on the grounds that they threaten 'current knowledge', rather than as contributions which might expand upon and perhaps even revolutionise thinking and practise in certain areas. However, the progress of ideas is not facilitated by the dead hand of orthodoxy and uniformity. I leave the reader to decide in which category to place the present offering.

Basically, this book seeks to extend the arguments of *The Myth of Addiction* by looking more closely at certain methodological and theoretical problems raised by that earlier work. The proposed methodological solution borrows heavily from the theory and methods of signal detection where analogous problems of dealing with variability in verbal reports are tackled via the notion of 'criterion for response'. A loosely analogous theory and method of 'social criterion analysis' is proposed, within which the verbal responses obtained in any individual data collection exercise are never viewed as definitive, but only as a sample taken from a range of such responses which vary according to the nature of the research method used. Any statement about what has been measured must thus be based on response variability over a range of settings, rather than on a fixed value obtained in only one.

However, a need is also identified for a principled and replicable method of dealing with naturalistic discourse within the context of minimally-cued conversations, that avoids the arbitrariness and selective excesses of some qualitative research, without resorting once more to the mortmain of forced-choice questionnaire bashing. This, it seems to me, is a major gap in the methodological armoury of the social researcher; the notion that qualitative and quantitative methods, separated by veritable philosophical chasms, can simply be cobbled together side by side within the same research exercise simply will not do (Davies, 1996). In an attempt to bridge this gap, a framework for dealing with minimally structured conversations is suggested, based on the idea that the natural history of drug use is reflected in various recognisable *types* of functional discourse, produced by drug users at different stages of their drug-use careers. Within the proposed system, however, it is not necessary to make any assumptions about the 'real meaning' or 'truthfulness' of any piece of discourse. Our data show that the types of conversations described are certainly recognisable by others with a reasonable degree of consensus. They may also relate in a loose way to certain indices of outcome, though more evidence is required on this point.

There is a long way to go however, and the thing we are working towards appears at the present time as a large beast in a fog. Different parts become visible from time to time; but they often disappear again under extended scrutiny, and there is no clear idea of what the whole beast looks like. Perhaps the fog will clear if we persevere long enough. Whilst those of us involved in the hunt have no clear idea where we shall end up, and the evidence is suggestive rather than convincing, we shall follow this beast since we are in no doubt that there is something interesting out there. We hope that others may join the pursuit.

I would like to thank some friends, all of whom I believe struggle with these issues, for help, support, enthusiasm, new ideas (sometimes blinding and sometimes off-the-wall), and also a hint of madness. They are David Best, Steve McCarthy, Nick Heather, Fiona McConnachie, Doug Cameron, Ron McKechnie, Peter Cohen, David Shewan and Freek Polak. I owe particular thanks to Maria Crugeira and Linda Wright for restoring coherence to a data analysis that seemed likely to lose its way for a brief period. I would also wish to thank many others who, whilst possibly not sharing my views, have taken time on various occasions to discuss these ideas with me, and who have sometimes said something that has stuck in my mind, often over a period of several years. They include Ernie Drucker, Michael Gossop, Ray Hodgson, Bill Saunders, Mary McMurran, Jim Orford, Ian Hindmarch, Dick Eiser, Robert West, John Strang, Charles Lind, Bruce Ritson, Jonathon Potter, Judy Greenwood and many others. I am especially indebted to David Best and Maria Crugeira for major contributions to the development of the discursive model described in the latter sections of this book. Finally, I wish to thank the Scottish Office for funding a number of projects which collectively have given rise to the line of thinking described in the following pages.

And I concede that I was wrong about the rabbit, but that's as far as I am prepared to go!

1

Explaining Addiction

The ideas put forward in this book derive from two sources. Firstly, in the book, *The Myth of Addiction*, certain arguments from the general area of attribution theory were applied to the verbal responses and behaviour of people normally referred to as "drug addicts". It was argued that central to popular and lay beliefs, but also at the heart of some more expert accounts, is the idea that "addiction" changes the basis for human behaviour. The assumption is that "non-addicted" people have control over their behaviour in ways that "addicted" people do not. Whether one conceptualises this distinction as the presence or absence of "free will," or as due to the presence or absence of a pharmacologically-driven compulsion deriving from the drug ingested, makes no difference to the description advocated. The keystone to the addiction debate is the idea that "non-addicted" behaviour is "free" in some way that "addicted" behaviour is not. This alleged but impossible distinction is signalled in the discourse of addiction primarily through the use of terms such as "compulsion" and "loss of control", which by implication contrast with the non-compelled and controlled behaviour of those who are "not addicted".

The *Myth of Addiction* argued that, notwithstanding the fact that some people encounter terrible problems as a consequence of their unwise use of drugs, any supposed shift in the principles underlying their behaviour is a myth (or to be more precise, a functional social construction); no such change takes place and indeed such a shift is philosophically untenable and empirically non-demonstrable.

A major source of information on this supposed shift from

mediated to compelled behaviour is the accounts that "addicts" themselves provide about their own behaviour; in other words, the things they say when asked to explain why they perform certain acts. From an attributional standpoint, such explanations are seen as socially functional accounts rather than veridical or "scientific" explanations. Because of the social and legal situations that drug users frequently find themselves in, it makes sense for them to describe their behaviour as non-volitional. Indeed, in a very real sense, being "addicted" means finding oneself in a situation where it is necessary to talk like an "addict" in order to survive. In the *Myth of Addiction* it was also argued that repeatedly finding oneself in situations where one has to rehearse and repeat such explanations increases the likelihood that one's behaviour will tend to change over time in order to fit with the stereotype of the "helpless addict" that one is repeatedly forced to endorse; and research into the attributional aspects of behaviour suggests a mechanism whereby socially functional explanations can come true at the end of the day. The mechanisms for this lie within the area of "attributional theory", a central notion of which is that the explanations one adopts have implications for future behaviour.

However, there is a second and much broader set of issues which motivates this present text. In the course of many studies examining the functional nature of verbal reports (that is the way in which people's accounts of themselves vary according to the situation they find themselves in) the author and some close colleagues have become increasingly concerned about a number of the standard methodologies which psychologists use for dealing with verbal behaviour. Consequently, the use of questionnaires as a means of finding out "truth" has become for us an increasingly unsatisfying exercise, and the use of check-lists or forced-choice procedures to "measure" entities inside the head has started to seem an increasingly unlikely enterprise. Perhaps most of all, the very distinction between "true" and "false" as revealed in verbal behaviour of any kind appears to be bedevilled with both philosophical and practical problems; and the use of statistical and psychometric procedures designed to ensure that tests produce "truth" has started to appear like some dangerous self delusion that actually cuts straight across any notion of verbal behaviour as motivated, functional and symbolic (Davies, 1996). To the extent that psychology makes widespread use of such methods in pursuit of "truth", large areas of psychological inquiry come under scrutiny and the results are disquieting. It is reassuring to note, however, that certain other writers feel much the same; Maynard for example has suggested (1990) that questionnaires can "produce a falsely concrete body of data which distorts rather than reflects actor's meanings".

By contrast, this text suggests that alternative philosophies and methods may offer pointers to the direction in which a new type of psychological inquiry might proceed with respect to verbal behaviour. In the following pages, a theory and an associated method are described for dealing with the natural discourse produced by drug users at various points in their careers. This account, however, represents only an isolated attempt to describe the nature of discourse within a particular area, namely drug use. We believe that a similar approach could be used in any behavioural domain, to provide an analysis of the natural history of functional discourse within a particular legal, social and economic context. By adopting such an approach, by abandoning certain methodological rigours which now appear to us as scientistic rather than scientific, and by replacing them with others which are more appropriate to the symbolic, interactional and functional nature of conversation, we believe that a more useful account can be obtained. We believe that the future of psychology requires the development and testing of new methods with new theoretical underpinnings, rather than the repeated application of accepted wisdoms about what constitutes "scientific research" and particularly "psychological measurement" in areas which seem, to us, increasingly inappropriate.

Contemporary arguments about the nature of scientific enquiry, and the place of social science within that framework, date back at least to the 1940s. However, in more recent times trains of reasoning and thought deriving from logical positivism and materialism, and systems of self-regulating scientific progress as outlined by Popper (1959) have increasingly come under challenge. Nonetheless, this is the broad school of scientific philosophy and method from which mainstream "psychology-as-a-science" still draws its inspiration, and it is a matter for regret that such fixed concepts of science, coupled to a scientistic view of mind, still inform much psychological and other research in the present day. The notion of addiction as the manifestation of an independent or "extra-human" mechanism that submerges and over-rides normal human processes, and controls as if from a different locus the behaviour of the person showing the "condition", is just such an example. Unfortunately, the logic is deeply and obviously flawed, and it is a matter for regret that such an impossible concept is still researched with all seriousness in the name of "science".

If one is a determinist, all behaviour is determined. If one is a materialist, all behaviour is underlaid by tangible mechanism. "Free will" enters into neither of these pictures and is the territory of the phenomenologist and the existentialist. Yet the "scientific" view of substance abuse as "addiction" invites us to differentiate between people who are able to make decisions about a particular form of behaviour, and those who cannot exercise such powers. It is the opinion of the author that such an idea is basically unscientific, insofar as it violates certain principles of parsimony that scientists insist on as being defining principles of their own modes of procedure. This is a comment on both the concept of addiction, and on a prevailing concept of science in general, and psychology in particular.

In 1964, Sigmund Koch wrote:-

> ". . . . the emerging redefinition of knowledge is already at a phase, in its understanding of the particularities of inquiry, which renders markedly obsolete that view of science still regulative of inquiring practice in psychology" (p. 5)

and later

> ". . . . the view in question was imported, with undisguised gratitude, from the philosophy of science and related sources some three decades ago but, while remaining more or less congealed in psychology, was subjected to such attrition in the areas of its origin that in those areas it can no longer properly be said to exist. Psychology is thus in the unenviable position of standing on philosophical foundations which began to be vacated by philosophy almost as soon as the former had borrowed them". (p. 5)

According to this view, psychology has borrowed and enthusiastically applied the notions and methods of a naive view of physical science (and continues to do so) at precisely the time those views were being superseded at the grassroots of the physical sciences themselves. Alone in the scholarly community, he suggests, psychology remains dedicated to the pursuit of knowledge through a simplistic application of materialist and logical-positivist ideas and assumptions; ground which has since been vacated by the very subjects that psychology originally borrowed the ideas from.

However, Koch's assertion that only psychology suffers from this malaise may be overly optimistic. The basic problems of the nature of knowledge and the status of truth involve philosophical issues of a fundamental nature, which have been discussed by Locke, Hulme, Wittgenstein, Descartes, Nietzsche, Mill, Foucault, Derrida and many others. Unfortunately, their writings frequently fail to impinge on psychology or science degree courses to any marked extent (or indeed, at all in many cases), and thus we find ourselves in a strange position whereby alternative philosophies of knowledge, and more specifically of science, may be largely unfamiliar to many of its practitioners. Unencumbered by this body of literature, it thus apparently remains possible for researchers to plunge ahead with the disinterested and objective search for truth despite serious epistemological problems with the two central definers (i.e. "objective" and "disinterested") and with the nature of the central concept ("truth"). This perhaps has a minimal effect on the ability to carry out "scientific" research, but has more far-reaching and serious consequences for the status and implications that become attached to what is "found out".

In fairness, it should be pointed out that certain of the writers referred to in the above paragraph appear to be past masters at creating more problems than they solve; and also, at times, of expressing what are important but essentially easily-communicable ideas in the most flowery and opaque language. Furthermore, the philosophy of language which sees it (language) as devoid of absolute meaning, and as possessing significance only in a given context, is at the end of the day a disappointment to anyone who thought there were such things as informed opinions or expert views of the world. In the present text, a way out of this dilemma is tentatively suggested which does no major violence to contemporary philosophies of language (though it admittedly does some minor violence) whilst still admitting the utility of asking sensible questions and the possibility of producing useful answers whose epistemological roots are different, and in some ways arguably less individually subjective, than opinions produced in everyday linguistic contexts. *The central theme of this book is that such a process is both conceivable and performable, and that the dilemmas proposed by a theory of discourse-bound-by-context are themselves not absolute. Consequently, it is still possible to distinguish between discourses which are primarily (but not exclusively) performative, and those which are primarily (but not exclusively) informative.*

However, an awareness of the underlying issues is essential to anyone calling themselves a scientist, since the arguments in question have the most profound implications for the way science is carried out, and particularly for any branch of science that makes use of verbal reports. At the end of the day, progress is only made by repeatedly throwing out old ways of conceptualising the world, by creating new frameworks for activity, and by developing new methodological paradigms, so a view of science that permits such re-construction to take place is an essential ingredient of what we like to call scientific progress. By contrast, if at some (any) point in time we presume we have discovered "the truth" about a particular set of phenomena, what need is there for any more research? There is nothing new to find out! (see for example Lawson & Appignanesi, 1989). However, even a cursory glance at the history of science shows that today's "truth", whether it concerns the flatness of the earth, the motions of the planets, phlogiston, or quarks, is invariably replaced by something else. Consequently a struggle to preserve present-day "knowledge" is always misconceived, is essentially anti-progress, and may be more a sign of insecurity and territorial defence than anything else.

The basic illogicality of the notion of addiction, which brings the exclusive worlds of mechanism and free will into straightforward collision, and then claims that this has actual explanatory value in scientific terms, is a concrete example of a construct which is preserved for its social functionality, despite its lack of scientific coherence and the philosophical incompatibility that lies at its core. It also illustrates the basic and still-resounding dilemma in psychology; how to come to terms with mind within a philosophy that asserts that there is only matter. Or, if you prefer a behaviourist interpretation, how to describe volition within a system that only admits environmental vectors. At some point we have to come to terms with these fundamentally different but equally significant ways of thinking about human action, and of clarifying for ourselves that level at which we wish to speak, and for what purpose. The concept of addiction is a barrier to progress, since it confuses these issues at the very outset. Perhaps it is time it went the way of all scientific ideas, whether about the flatness of the earth, the earth as the centre of the universe, phlogiston as the essence of matter, or in time (as sure as eggs appear to be eggs) quarks. Such concepts are always through-stations on the lines along which we travel in the practice of science (as we conceive of it), but none of them can be said to be the terminus.

If the above polemic has any merit at all, it can come as little surprise that the scientific study of addiction has made only modest progress when it comes to applying scientific theory to the actual day to day problems faced by those whose drug use is, for whatever, reason, problematic. On the one had, we have research at the micro level (physiology, pharmacology, biochemistry, neurology) which elucidates specific drug related effects on the brain, which have at best only the most oblique and tenuous explanatory power with respect to activities such as going down to the local pub for a pint of beer, or stealing a television to get money to pay for a fix of heroin. On the other hand, we have social research, which commits itself largely to prevalence (or head-counting exercises), supplemented by the atheoretical search for plausible, convenient and probably serendipitous relationships between who takes what drug, and a variety of social and demographic variables. This is usually followed by a brief statement indicating that such relationships do not necessarily indicate causality, followed by a lengthy discussion of their possible causal status!

The gulf between going down to the pub explained as an act of choice (however conceptualised) within a social and historical context, or in terms of (say) the adaptation of neurones in the reticular formation to repeated doses of a general anaesthetic, remains as vast as ever. According to choice, we either count the one, or measure the other, and shout abuse across the void about whose view is correct, or most correct; or most "true" or "scientific". For the time being, it is sufficient simply to point out that the sentence "The reason the man went to the pub was that he wanted a pint of beer" is philosophically distinct, and its implications quite different, from the sentence "The cause of the man's behaviour in going to the pub was alcohol", this despite the fact that either sentence could be said to describe the act in question honestly. But the first description implies choice whereas the second implies compulsion.

The way we conceptualise such phenomena is thus reflected in a very real way by the words we choose (decide to use) to describe it in the first place; and that choice is functional insofar as it sets the scene for whatever particular approach we already intend to bring to the problem. The choice of a particular research approach to the phenomenon of a man going to a pub depends not on any "scientific" principle, but reveals itself as an *a priori* judgement via the initial preference for one sentence rather than the other as the preferred (i.e. "better", "more scientific", "truer") description of the act from the outset. And this in turn derives from our own learning histories which encapsulate the kind of expertise we wish to bring to bear. What is clear, though, is that the answers one obtains from the chosen method will address only certain types of question, and do little justice to other ways of conceptualising the problem.

The limited utility of addressing a physiological or pharmacological issue in social terms is usually apparent (for example, explaining the function of the reticular formation in terms of social class) but what is more difficult to understand is why answering a socially constituted question in pharmacological terms should be any more sensible. The latter can only be seen as "more sensible" from a standpoint that views (in this case) the pharmacological explanation as superordinate to another (or any other) type of explanation. That is, as in principle "better", "truer" or "more real". In fact, however, such a standpoint is implicit in "reductionism", which in a sense seeks to represent "the ultimate truth" underlying all matter and all existence. We should remember though that reductionism is *in itself* philosophically derived; not scientifically. It is not provable by science, but only defensible in terms of deductive (non-empirical) reasoning. As such, people can disagree with the premises underlying it, as with any other idea based on certain *a priori* assumptions. Any scientist claiming a superior status for his/her particular brand of reductionist epistemology is thus unfamiliar with the basic building blocks of the trade; that is, with the philosophy of science.

Whilst the absence of an integrated theory of addiction remains as stark a reality as ever, this book represents a second attempt to reconceptualise the notion of addiction as a motivated species of discourse. Briefly, it is argued that drug use becomes addiction when a person who uses drugs finds him/herself in situations where it is necessary to talk like an "addict" in order to survive. Such situations are defined in terms of factors which are pharmacological, social, economic and legal in origin, although the state of "addiction" *per se* inheres in none of these areas. Within such a system, issues of freewill or compulsion, or pharmacological versus social determinism, are sterile; whilst the search for the "causes" of addiction as a state are doomed to failure, since the search is in fact for a mechanism underlying nothing more substantial than a learned and widely known set of functional figures of speech. However, it is the message of this book that the key to understanding drug problems requires an examination of how and when that figure of speech becomes necessary, and why it is so highly valued by drug users, their families, clinicians, and researchers alike. From such a viewpoint, "addiction" is not simply a state of a person; nor an inherent pharmacological property of drugs, nor an inevitable response to demographics although all these things play a part. It is a way of thinking (a "construct"), and it is the psychological consequence ("output") of a many faceted system. Furthermore, it is a property of that system as a whole, and is not defined wholly or partly by any individual element in that system. However, the final essential piece of the addiction jigsaw puzzle slots into place when the user starts talking about him/herself in a particular way, in order to reduce the sanctions attendant on a disapproved-of form of behaviour. As we shall see in later chapters, once this decision has been made there is no way back and paradise, or at least a type of innocence with respect to drug use, is indeed lost forever.

"Addiction" then, it is argued, is a way of talking and behaving which is adaptive for drug users who encounter problems within a system which places sanctions on this type of activity. In a different setting "it" might not exist, or might exist in some other form. To search for "it" as an entity that resides inside people, or inside substances, is to basically misunderstand the problem. As long the notion of "addiction" has at its core the basic requirement to flit between two (volitional versus non-volitional) types of explanation which are non-complementary, or worse, to imagine that volitional and non-volitional are opposite poles of a continuum (so that free will becomes a matter of degree) we can expect to continue chasing our tails for the foreseeable future.

The present text seeks to suggest possible ways out of this hall of mirrors. A method is suggested for dealing with the things that drug users tell drug workers, which makes no assumptions about the truth or falsity of the accounts offered, but seeks to examine their functionality within a drug use career. The result is a kind of natural history of drug discourse, in which the kinds of explanations, stories and narratives offered by drug users are seen to change and evolve in predictable ways over the course of a drug using career, as they adapt to changing circumstances. The driving force for these explanations, stories and narratives is assumed to be their adaptive utility in a sequence of evolving and changing contexts surrounding drug use, and therefore, the ability to recognise particular features of the narratives would, in principle, give a guide to the kinds of situations currently being encountered by the rapporteur. The "truthfulness" of the accounts is unknowable, as with *all* verbal reports but furthermore, in the context of the present method, it is unimportant.

Finally, it is the intention and hope that the analysis of the discourse of drug users offered in this text will be simply one example of an approach which can be applied in other areas. By virtue of the changing dynamics of the situations in which they find themselves, drug users comprise a crucial study group, insofar as the functionality of their conversations changes (we believe) in a known sequence, sometimes in a fairly short space of time. We do not believe, however that the dynamics of their conversations are fundamentally different from those of anyone else. In order to illustrate this point, the present text also offers a loose discursive analysis of some of the standard and more-or-less hallowed definitions offered by experts whose chosen vocation includes the treatment of those who are believed to be addicted. The aim is to show that the functional discursive phenomenon we have described as "drugspeak" (after Dally, 1990) characterises the utterances not only of users, but also of those who propose therapeutic means of influencing that use. We believe that whilst the functionality of both discourses is in principle identifiable, objectivity or "truth" cannot be assumed to reside in either. However, this does not mean that progress cannot be made.

2

Drug Taking and The Laws of Nature

Whilst at a detailed level there are many different theories of "addiction", most of the differences are superficial rather than fundamental. A central feature is the desire to distinguish between addicted behaviour and non-addicted behaviour, coupled to a preference for explaining the former in terms of physical and pharmacological processes (laws of nature), and the latter in terms of volition and intentionality. Thus, to be addicted is to be "compelled"; whereas compulsion is not seen as a feature of "non-addicted" behaviour. This distinction remains at the heart of virtually all theories of addiction, and thus identifies them as theoretical "isotopes" rather than new theories. In the following chapter it is argued that this dominant theory, and hence all its variants or isotopes, is based on a flawed philosophy of science, and that consequently there is ample room for genuine theoretical innovation.

Debates about the notion of addiction, whether "it" is a disease or not, whether people's regular repetitive actions with respect to psychoactive substances are volitional or compelled, and whether scientists will sooner or later find the mechanism that underlies such behaviour (and thereby the "magic bullet" that will "cure" it) are merely microcosms of ethical and philosophical debates that have troubled thinkers for centuries. However, researchers who specialise in a particular field sometimes become preoccupied, a not unnatural occurrence when people find fascination in a particular research topic. This means however that a kind of "tunnel vision" can develop, whereby awareness of relevant issues in other fields is sacrificed. This may have happened with research into addiction where there is sometimes a lack of awareness that

11

issues central to addiction are not specific to that area. To some extent the tricky questions, perhaps imponderables, that trouble addiction workers have troubled others in various guises since the dawn of recorded history. Consequently the arguments that ensue often have a familiar feel to them; they tend to keep popping up like old friends and bad pennies. In effect, "the flat tyre keeps being reinvented time after time" (a quote for which I am indebted to Professor Keith Tones, of Leeds Metropolitan University) with respect to central issues about the nature of addiction.

The classification of an aspect of human existence as a "disease" arises not so much from any compelling unity in the principles underlying the class of phenomena so labelled as from a unity in how we intend to conceptualise and deal with the phenomenon at a societal level. If something is a "disease", then the remedy lies in some form of "treatment" since the phenomenon is defined by the "disease" label as pathological or "abnormal". It is clear to see, however, that a consensus definition of disease is probably easier to apply, and fits less awkwardly, in cases such as pneumonia or influenza where an invading causal agent can be isolated, than in cases such as dyslexia, attention deficit disorder (ADD) and attention deficit hyperactivity disorder (ADHD) where the aetiology is more debatable, and where viewing the associated behaviours as abnormal or pathological raises value-laden and ethical, as well as purely scientific and medical, questions. See Davies (1993) for a discussion of the dyslexia issue; also *The Psychologist* (1995) for discussions of ADD/ADHD.

"Disease" definitions also raise problems with respect to the presence or absence of "free will", and thus can provoke collision between volitional accounts of human action and alternative accounts based on materialist, reductionist and hence determinist philosophies that underly much of what we refer to as "scientific knowledge". Calling something a "disease" carries an important social message, not just a medical one. It implies that the phenomenon itself is not brought about directly by the individuals who display it; though they may of course put themselves more or less at risk by their "voluntary" actions. Thus AIDS (the disease) is not brought about because people deliberately produce a deficiency in their immune systems; even though their actions with respect to sexual practices, or injecting drug use, may be seen to have a bearing on whether they acquire the disease. In a similar way mountaineers do not deliberately choose to suffer from cerebral oedema, even though they choose to climb to heights where this condition is more likely to come about. Nonetheless, a disease is not usually conceptualised in itself as having a voluntary basis, and consequently the label removes personal responsibility from the individual who therefore merits "treatment". It is this implied removal of personal responsibility which makes "disease" notions so popular and attractive in social cognitive terms. If something is a disease, the individual "sufferer" cannot be blamed for it. The value of the label is thus substantial, and so we witness a relentless widening in the use of the concept, bringing in more and more problems under its protective canopy even though the fit between some of these and a commonsense notion of disease becomes increasingly loose. Are we really expected to take the alleged condition "shopaholism" seriously? And if so, who is next in the queue (no pun intended) to have responsibility for their own ill-considered actions removed by the wonders of science?

An analogous debate has raged for some decades over homosexual behaviour, where once again disease/genetic arguments collide with conceptions based on choice, despite the fact that where multi-determined and molar behaviours are concerned there is nothing contradictory about acknowledging that both arguments can have value in particular contexts. One is clearly free to choose whether to carry out many behaviours which have been shown to have a genetic or hereditary component. For example in *The Naked Civil Servant* (Crisp, 1985), an autobiographical work describing the life of Quentin Crisp, the author describes the problems created by a homosexual lifestyle at a time when such behaviour was against the law in the U.K. The central character is at one point asked to tell the court how long he has suffered from homosexuality. He replies that he has been homosexual for many years, but he ironically questions the appropriateness of the term "suffering from". In a similar vein, those of us who can remember the days when homosexual activity was illegal may also remember media coverage of certain scandals, within which reference to homosexual behaviour as a "condition" that people "suffered from" was the norm. The author even recalls a popular science programme about "cures" for this condition based on aversion therapy (electric shock), which featured a number of people who had been arrested for homosexual acts, and who had consequently "volunteered" for the new "treatment".

Nowadays, such a view would be seen by most of us as homophobic and unwarranted. Subsequent changes in the law meant that it was no longer necessary to plead illness when such behaviour came to light, and consequently there was no longer any drive to have it "treated". Homosexuals of both genders now can "come out" and present their sexual behaviour in an open and positive light; stressing choice and personal preference (Assiter & Carol, 1993; Carol, 1994) as the main motives; and few if any feel a need to sign up for electric-shock aversion therapy in order to be "cured". The status of homosexual behaviour as the manifestation of disease, and the conclusion that treatment was an appropriate disposal, can thus be seen with hindsight to have depended crucially on the position of that behaviour with regard to the law, notwithstanding the wealth of scientific journal articles attesting to the physical and genetic bases of the "condition". It is argued here that, in a similar way, the legislation surrounding drug use places a premium on deterministic explanations to which people would need less recourse in a different judicial climate. In both these cases, the legal status of the activity appears to determine the preferred mode of explanation.

The debate about whether drug users use drugs volitionally because they want to, or whether the behaviour is compelled by forces beyond the individual's control, also has a philosophical origin. However, the issue cannot be resolved by "science", unless science itself is viewed as a way of finding absolute truth, rather than a convenient way of conceptualising the world which helps in the solving of particular types of problems. The reasons for conceptualising something as a disease, particularly in grey areas like addiction, or dyslexia, are primarily social and functional; yet these labels can apparently be "proved to exist" by scientific data which in one way or another show what the underlying physiological mechanism is. However, from a reductionist point of view all behaviour has an underlying mechanism. Thus, if it became necessary to re-conceptualise road crossing as a "disease" (suppose for example that it was made illegal, but numbers of high-status people persisted in doing it) we could confidently expect our scientists to "prove" its disease status by identifying, or at least suggesting, an underlying mechanism; for there surely is one, or else we would be unable to cross the road.

Furthermore, once the underlying mechanism had been revealed, we might anticipate the supremely illogical announcement that the scientific data showed the behaviour to be non-volitional or "compulsive" on the precise grounds that a mechanism had been identified. It remains a mystery why the fact of finding, unsurprisingly, that a behaviour has an underlying mechanism should be taken as conclusive evidence that the behaviour is not volitional. In fact, the philosophy behind science as mechanism is simply that, basically, everything is underlain by a tangible mechanism or process. This is not unreasonable. In principle, however, such a philosophical stance has nothing to say on the issue of volition. It can neither confirm nor disconfirm volitional theories; and it certainly cannot discriminate between volitional and non-volitional acts.* The emergence of this problem with respect to drug use is however simply the re-emergence in a specific area of a centuries old debate about the sources of human action; it is nothing new.

The third issue arising from the opening paragraph of this section concerns the ways in which scientists construe the work that they do. The preferred and widely held notion of science sees it as the pursuit of some ultimate truth by individuals whose actions are free from motive, ideology or favour. Skinner for example writes, "Science is a search for order, for uniformities, for lawful relation among the events of nature"; and also "If we are to use the methods of science in the field of human affairs, we must assume that behaviour is lawful and determined..." (Skinner, 1953; Machan, 1974). It is worthwhile noting specifically that Skinner carefully avoids claiming that the theory of operant behaviour "proves" the lawfulness or determinist nature of human behaviour. That is, he acknowledges, an assumption ("we must assume that behaviour is lawful and determined.") that has to be made before his theory of human action can be applied.

To take another example, an editorial in the influential journal *Addiction* commences with the assertion, "Science is at its best the selfless and disinterested pursuit of truth" (Edwards *et al.*, 1995). The assumptions underlying these two quotes, namely that a) human action is underlaid by laws that parallel, and are

---

*The conclusion that demonstration of a mechanism is sufficient to render an act non-volitional only makes sense in conjunction with a parallel but unarticulated assumption; namely that volitional acts are NOT so underlaid. This, of course, runs contrary to the basic mechanistic assumption that everything is underlaid by mechanism. (I am indebted to Prof Michael Bozarth for the amazing, possibly ironic, quote, "One day we will understand the pharmacology of free will." Florence, 1989, verbal communication whilst standing with the author at the bar). If on the other hand it is the contention that there is no such thing as volition, or that volition is delusional or epiphenomenological (the mere experience of "the machine working") then the mechanist may not use words such as "compulsive" to distinguish one set of behaviours from another, since he invokes a dimension in which he does not believe.

in fact nothing more than instances of, the kinds of laws underlying the events of nature (i.e. physical laws); and b) that scientists are the selfless and disinterested pursuers of the ultimate truths underlying these laws, probably coincide rather well with the self perceptions of many practising scientists. But if so then the matter is one for regret rather than congratulation. The sentiments are laudable, but they reveal a disregard for (or dismissal of?) alternative contemporary philosophies of knowledge in general and science in particular; and perhaps also a potentially dangerous misunderstanding of the place of the scientist within society insofar as the idea is perpetrated that science proceeds untouched by human motivation. "Therefore", it comprises a body of value-free knowledge, and this warrants its privileged and superordinate ("more true") epistemological status vis a vis other forms of knowledge – this raises a number of issues which are, at the very least, worthy of acknowledgment.

In order to explore these stormy waters further, let us commence with a brief examination of the idea that laws can be found underlying human action that parallel "the laws of nature". The sport of boxing, let it be acknowledged, is not to everyone's taste. It is possible to argue the case in favour of boxing, in terms of people's rights to do what they wish just as long as they do so in full awareness of the possible consequences of their actions, and provided no-one else's liberty to do likewise is interfered with. This is basically the philosophy put forward by Mill in 1859 (cited in Friedman & Szasz, 1992) and it remains a viable principle for the organisation of a society to the present day. The basis for Mill's argument is captured in the much-cited essay *On Liberty*, in which he states, "The only purpose for which power can be rightfully exercised over any member of a civilised community, against his will, is to prevent harm to others."

On the other hand, Mill also conceded that a breach of duty to others could constitute "harm" as envisioned in the above quotation, giving rise thereby to arguments above definitions of "duty". It is possible to argue that boxers fail in their duty to their families and dependents by risking injury in the boxing ring; but the same argument then applies to any risky occupation, including deep-sea oil exploration, grand-prix racing and, until recently, coal mining. All these activities, whilst involving risk, also actually constitute the very means by which people provide for their families and dependents. However, the real health consequences of boxing are a cause of serious concern, and it can be argued that the sport should be banned precisely for those reasons, regardless of whether people wish to take part or not. The good (freedom) of individuals in a society is thus, arguably, not the same as the common good of the society as a whole, and so interventions that violate individual freedoms are justified at the societal level in terms of a greater common good (Beauchamp, 1987). In a sense, these arguments, involving pitting freedom of individual choice against the need to serve the interests of the broader society at large parallel quite closely some of the arguments about drug prohibition versus legalisation, the pro- and anti- boxing argument, the annual death toll of climbers in the Grampians of Scotland, and a number of other areas of activity where the exercise of individual freedoms, whilst not seriously infringing the rights of other specified individuals to do as they wish, nonetheless imposes a cost on the society as a whole.

However one feels about boxing, perhaps we may agree that Muhammed Ali was arguably the greatest, most skilled and most charismatic exponent of the boxing arts ever to grace (or if you prefer, disgrace) the surface of the planet; and it is a matter of fact and regret that he has paid the final terrible price for his choice of vocation. Ali, it may be recalled, took part in a number of legendary confrontations with chat show hosts as well as in the boxing ring. In one such unattributed incident, it is alleged that Ali was asked to explain *why* he became a boxer.

Questions beginning with "why" are of special interest to psychologists, particularly "attribution theorists" whose interest lies in trying to understand why people choose the types of explanations they do, when asked to explain their behaviours. This approach assumes, on the basis of substantial evidence, that people's explanations for their behaviour are not simple causal accounts, but cognitive constructions that take into account the circumstances in which the explaining is to take place. From an attributional perspective, Ali's answer was not disappointing. After a moment's thought, he intoned the following three line epithet in his own inimitable sing-song style:-*

"The bird flies through the air.
The waves pound on the seashore.

---

*authors note:- I can remember distinctly reading an account of this incident somewhere, but it is one of the unwritten rules of authorship that, at the end of the day, you will be unable to find the reference for the most crucial and interesting thing that you come across. However, in this instance I am not going to be deterred by such a mere detail.

I beat people up."

This brilliant piece of improvisation was greeted with gales of laughter and applause, and rightly so. The collision of two matrices of meaning (Koestler, 1964) is self evident.

However, whilst fully accepting that the psychological analysis of jokes is one of the world's more boring and unimaginative enterprises, it now becomes necessary to try to answer the question, "Why is it funny?", in order to illustrate the point that is being made. So what is it that collides with what in Ali's hilarious and ridiculous riposte?

The structure of a bird, its wings, its bones, its musculature, have developed as a consequence of the operation of biological laws outlined in the theory of evolution and captured in adaptive genes. Flying requires certain kinds of structure. It is not simply the case that birds decide to fly according to some whim, whilst other animals do not. Birds fly because they have evolved the genetic make-up that makes flying the best way to get about for birds. Birds fly because that is what they do; what they are designed for. "The bird flies through the air" is a statement of biological fact deriving from the operation of laws of nature.

Waves pound on the seashore for reasons concerning gravity, the pull that larger bodies exert on smaller ones; and the action of the winds deriving from peturbations of the atmosphere as the planet wobbles on its axis. The gravitational force exerted primarily by the moon tugs the oceans about in a fashion that is predictable from a knowledge of gravity and of the moon, and the winds whip up the surface from time to time in a less predictable but nonetheless determined manner. These things happen as a consequence of the operation of physical laws of nature.

Mohammed Ali's epithet is funny because he ironically implies that his boxing is a law of nature also. We are invited to believe that he boxed because he was expressly designed to do so, as in the case of the bird that flies; and because he had no choice in the matter, as when the waves pound on the beach. He asks us to consider that he boxed due to the operation of laws that transcend human decision making. This is funny, because we know that such an explanation is inappropriate and unhelpful; that a more informative explanation would give greater prominence to social circumstances and early life history, opportunities, business deals, motives, aspirations, situations, personal perceptions, luck, and decision making. In terms of Koestler's analysis therefore, our "laws of nature" matrix collides with our "human beings as sentient decision makers" matrix, and the result is humour. According to Koestler, *if we felt the idea, that Ali's behaviour was caused by universal laws, was reasonable and appropriate, WE WOULD NOT FIND IT FUNNY.*

It is worthwhile pursuing Ali's ironic explanation with a more homely, hypothetical example. Suppose that whilst walking down the street we observe a woman frantically waving her arms about. Let it be further supposed that as students of human behaviour, we are sufficiently intrigued by her behaviour to ask why she is acting in such a way. Now imagine our surprise if, in response to the question she replies in terms of transmission of neurochemicals to receptor sites, innervation of motor neurones, conversion of sugars into lactic acid within muscles, levels of dopamine in the meso-acumbens, or other physiological factors that might well be involved in arm waving. How would we react to such an answer?

It is clear that *within a social context,* such an explanation would be quite uninformative as an explanation for the behaviour which is clearly a motivated social act. It conveys no sense of purpose, has no social relevance, and might in all probability be seen as deliberate *refusal* to provide an explanation in any circumstance other than a physiology laboratory. On the other hand, "My Mother is on the other side of the street", a simple statement of fact, has total explanatory power within that context, explaining as it does the purpose of the act; that is, the reason why "the organism" (she) behaved as it (she) did.

Explaining some motivated act in terms of a "law of nature" is thus not only funny in certain situations (as has hopefully been illustrated above). It can also be totally unhelpful within anything resembling a social context, and can in principle provide no evidence for differentiating one person's behaviour from another's; we are all subject to laws of nature. However, choosing to explain the actions of a subset of the human population (for example, "addicts' ") in terms of laws of nature is not merely unhelpful in individual terms; it is also illogical. It can only claim any discriminatory value by comparison with a group of people to whom those universal laws do not apply. Thus, to suggest that "addicts' " behaviour is determined by laws of the universe at a physiological, neurological, biochemical, or pharmacological level only has value if we can assume that a similar type of determinist explanation cannot be applied to the rest of us.

In fact, of course, we can choose to describe everyone's behaviour in these socially irrelevant terms if we so wish. From a reductionist /determinist viewpoint, all behaviour is "caused" (determined) by factors at this micro-level. Consequently, the supposed "compulsive" nature of addiction is not an empirically derived scientific finding; it is an *a priori* assumption underlying much of the research to which reductionist/mechanistic philosophies give rise. And as we have seen, such an assumption is quite unwarranted. If you prefer mechanistic explanations for behaviour, you are certainly entitled to them, and you can surely find mechanisms that underly any behaviour that people perform if you so wish. But what you can never do is provide evidence to support a theory that requires a distinction between "compulsive" and "non-compulsive" *mechanisms*. Unless you live in hopes of one day demonstrating the mechanism that underlies free will!

However, whether or not our research assumptions are well or ill-founded, they still have important implications. An important feature of contrasting explanations in terms of laws of nature as opposed the explanations in terms that have social relevance, is that they can both be true within a scientific conception of "truth". If the woman who was waving her arms about chooses to explain her actions in terms of the neurology, biochemistry and physiology of her anatomy, she is not telling lies. But what she is doing is offering an explanation of a type which is mismatched to the purpose of the question (e.g. "Why are you waving your arms about?"). Within the context described, such an answer could only make sense as a deliberate refusal to answer the question; a desire not to reveal the motive for the behaviour. Consequently, the answer is completely unhelpful with respect to understanding the social relevance of the behaviour. Furthermore, it would lead us to suppose, in an imaginary world in which arm waving was viewed as a problem behaviour or "disease", that the appropriate "treatment" also lay at a physiological, neurological or biochemical level, rather than in terms of the lady's mother and the presence of a busy street. We could provide the lady with medication or perhaps even surgery to stop her arms moving; or we could build a zebra crossing.

It should by now be plain that scientists choose their preferred type of explanation to suit the type of knowledge they possess, and advocate the policies and interventions most consistent with that knowledge. This of course is a very long way from the "selfless and disinterested pursuit of truth" described earlier. Furthermore, the processes by which scientists find themselves searching for the physiological mechanisms underlying drug-taking rather than, say, the physiological mechanisms of standing for parliament are very much social and political, and scientists ignore cultural, political and historical factors at their peril. It has been argued elsewhere that defining oneself as a selfless and disinterested searcher after truth is to lay oneself open to manipulation by those who harbour no such conceits (Machan *op. cit.*).

Muhammed Ali's joke is more than peripherally related to the prevailing concept of addiction. Addiction, we are invited to believe, is a "law of nature". People are addicted because their drug taking takes on the same status as birds flying (i.e. irresistable pharmacological/physiological forces that compel). People do not make decisions about their drug use. Instead of decision making, the word "addiction" invites us to view regular excessive drug use in terms of forces over which the person has no control. From such a position, they cannot behave otherwise. We might therefore offer the following as an answer to the question, "Why do you take drugs?"

The bird flies through the air.

The waves pound on the seashore.

I take heroin.

Suddenly, however, the irony is lost and no-one is laughing, though the absurdity of the explanation is identical in both cases. And meanwhile, in both the scientific and the popular literature, the terms "addiction" and "compulsive use" trip from pen and tongue as though there were no epistemological problems raised by the use of these terms. The idea that drug taking is a career and that, like boxing, it depends on circumstances, decisions, chance meetings, motives, business deals, opportunities, and so forth is relegated to a back seat. In its place a "law of the universe" is proposed by way of explanation; an explanation that Muhammed Ali used, in different circumstances, for the amusement of a chat-show audience.

3

Diagnostic Criteria: Scientific Definition or Functional Discourse?

The function of expert definitions

It is often assumed that expert or scientific writings are free of bias, free of hidden agendas or values, and "objective". In a sense, the assumption is that the actual words written are compelled by an inescapable logic such that anyone possessing the same facts or data would have written the same text in the same way. The scientific writer merely serves as a mouthpiece for arguments and conclusions that are inherent in the data, and the text itself is free from individual creativity, motive or intention deriving from an independent source within the writer. The present chapter, however, argues that none of this is in fact the case. Scientific writing is not concerned simply with the presentation of inescapable fact and conclusion, but with the skilled and edited presentation of material in such a way as to seduce the reader into accepting a particular argument rather than a different one, for reasons that may be personal, political, or whatever but are far from being dispassionate and disinterested. Science writing, like any other form of writing (including this book) is thus, first and foremost, functional.

In the introduction, the point was made that the discussion of the functional discourses of drug users which is undertaken primarily in chapters 6, 7 and 8 is to be complemented by an *ad hoc* analysis (to call it a content, discursive or qualitative analysis implies a degree of procedural rigour which it does not possess) of certain expert pronouncements on the condition known as addiction. The present chapter represents an attempt, therefore, to fulfil this commitment. The aim is to show that expert definitions invariably have at their core a) a number of terms which are ill-defined or undefined, b) a number of definitions which by a simple process of linguistic migration become explanations of the things for which they are only the definers, and c) a number of assumptions which are arbitrary, or matters of opinion rather than fact. In making this case, we have selected some of the best known and most influential compilations of diagnostic criteria to illustrate these points, not because they are especially bad, nor because their compilers are in some way "culpable". Indeed, in most respects they are the best criteria we have. They have been selected simply to illustrate the point that the problems described above can and do permeate even to the highest levels. The functional discourse of drugspeak is bi-directional; it comes from both sides of the fence and is mutually reinforcing. If the largely polemical arguments put forward can convince the reader even to a small degree that these problems do indeed exist, then the attempt will be considered worthwhile.

The need for definition

A characteristic of most scientific research studies is the emphasis placed on defining the central constructs and features of the research in a way that is clear and unambiguous. The need for definition arises due to the ambiguity inherent in many words as used in everyday speech; and also from the fact that scientists may sometimes use common terms in ways that do not reflect their everyday usage. For example, there would be little point in undertaking research into "depression", collecting data and disseminating findings, if the definition of "depression" was unclear. In such circumstances, and in the absence of a common definition of depression, the results would be either uninterpretable; or worse, would be open to misinterpretation if the readers' assumptions about what depression was did not reflect the scientists' assumptions. There must be, therefore, an agreed definition that is common to both the reader and the researcher, before the results can be meaningfully communicated. To the extent that there is no such consensus in terms of definition, there is scope for misunderstanding. People may imagine that they agree when they are actually talking about different things.

This is particularly likely in circumstances where the central construct is a word which occurs in everyday speech, and for which there exist strong societal expectations as to its meaning, but this meaning is not the one used by the experimenter. For example, research which employed a definition of the word "happiness" in terms of some physiological substrate, rather than a mood state, would be more prone to misinterpretation than a study employing an idiosyncratic use of the term "caco-. demonomania", since no general usage (and hence general understanding) of the latter exists.

The need for sensible definition

In order to overcome these difficulties, "operational definitions" are often used which have two purposes. Firstly, they aim to make it clear to the world at large what definition the researcher is working to. However, there is a second aspect to operational definition, arising from the fact that definitions are often made in terms of other objects or constructs which *themselves* require definition. For example, there is little point in trying to define a "bus" by reference to systems of public transport, large vehicles, wheels, internal combustion engines or whatever, if the recipient of this wisdom is as uncertain about the nature of public transport, vehicles, wheels, and engines as he/she is about buses.

In such circumstances, operational definition offers advantages, insofar as it seeks to define something, not in terms of *what it is like* (which threatens to introduce more unknown and undefined things into the definition) but rather in terms of performable and commonly understood operations. In the field of science such definition normally boils down to a description of *what you do to measure the thing in question*. According to the operationalist edict, "one can only understand a phenomenon to the extent that one can describe the techniques or procedures by which one is able to measure and study it" (Evans, 1978).

For example, the winner of a high-jump competition might be described as the "best jumper" or "the highest jumper", descriptions which are unsatisfactory since they leave room for confusion over terms such as "best", "highest" or even "jumper". For univocal definition it will thus be necessary to specify a standard system for the measurement of distance (feet, metres or whatever) and subsequently the necessity to suspend a horizontal bar at a known distance above the ground. Anyone propelling themselves solely by their own force over the bar without knocking it off its supports is then deemed to have "cleared" the height at the which the bar was last suspended. The winner is declared to be the one who "clears" the bar suspended at a greater height above the ground than any other competitor; and "clearing" requires only that the bar remain on its supports. A competitor who hits the bar without knocking it off is defined as having "successfully cleared" it for the purposes of high-jumping competitions.

We should note, however, that the operational definition of "successfully cleared" given above, whilst preserving its definitional status intact in terms of scientific exactitude, would be inappropriate in other settings. Suppose the hurdle to be cleared was a fence topped with sharp spikes? Suppose that a lethal high-voltage electrical current ran through it? In such circumstances one could be forgiven for saying something like the following:

> "I understand perfectly your definition of a successful clearance of the obstacle. Furthermore, in terms of that definition I am quite clear that the athlete has successfully cleared it. However, on the grounds that he is now lying in a crumpled and expiring heap on the other side, I find the phrase `successfully cleared' a strangely inappropriate form of words to describe what he just did."

It is thus quite possible to come up with an operational definition that flies in the face of common sense, or a least common usage. This is a problem where the idiosyncratic nature of the definition being employed by the scientist is not known to a larger section of the population who employ the common usage. This is especially the case where policy makers fall in the latter, rather than the former, group.

The opening paragraphs of this chapter are intended as an introduction to the problem of *definition as explanation*. Before proceeding further, however, it might be useful to summarise the problems of definition, especially where such definition makes use of words or terminology for which there already exist common understandings. Firstly, in the absence of definition, people may assume they understand each other when they are actually talking about different things. Secondly, where a definition exists but makes use of terms or constructs which are common in everyday speech people may assume, or continually regress to, a commonsense understanding which conflicts with a more esoteric definition being employed by the scientist. And thirdly, in the extreme case, a scientist may adopt a definition which conflicts with lay understandings to an extent which basically constitutes a misuse of the native language, whilst still being perfectly precise (one could, for example produce a perfectly unambiguous and precise operational definition of "white" in terms of the colour normally referred to as "black"). In such a case, and where the results of research become widely disseminated through the media, television and so forth but the fine detail is not similarly broadcast, public perceptions of what science has "proved" will be highly inaccurate.*

Explaining things "by definition"

Having touched on some of the problems of definition, it is now appropriate to turn to a more fundamental difficulty which compounds some of the problems described above. Relatively few workers in the area of addiction have been sufficiently bold to tackle this problem head on, but McMurran is one of these. She points out that definitions are sometimes used in the addiction literature *as if* they had explanatory value. Appropriately enough, she does this in a chapter on the phenomenon of "dependence".

With respect to dependence, McMurran (1994) writes;

> "Heavy involvement in an addictive behaviour, tolerance, withdrawal, compulsion and diminished control are all clinically observed phenomena. That is, certain people can be seen to experience them, or can tell you that they have these experiences. How then, may they be explained? In disease model terms, they are the defining features of dependence, which leads to a tautology. For example, an "addict" may say he or she craves the object of his or her addiction, and may be observed to indulge that craving by engaging in the addictive behaviour. Craving and loss of control are, thus, terms used to *describe* the person's behaviour. However, in order to *explain* these observations of craving and loss of control,

---

*The word "proved" is exactly a case in point. Whilst the lay public sees science as "proving" things, the definition of scientific "proof" is probabilistic and has little to do with everyday understandings of the word "proof" as a body of evidence which is in principle irrefutable.

the person is `diagnosed' as *dependent* upon the object of the addiction. Since the observations of craving and loss of control have been used to define dependence in the first place, the label `dependent' does nothing more than summarise these observations – there is no explanation of the observed behaviours attached to the `diagnosis'." (pp. 75-76)

In other words, a label is suggested in the first instance as a short-hand way of summarising a cluster of problem behaviours deriving from the use of certain substances. In this case, the behaviours are "the defining features of dependence", suggests McMurran. Subsequently, in a clinical context, a person who displays these behaviours is said to display them *because* he/she is dependent. Thus, the word "dependence" starts off as a summary descriptor for certain behaviours, and ends up in a clinical transaction as the explanation for the behaviours that define it.

The problem is that McMurran's comments with respect to dependence threaten to open a can of worms. Firstly, the way in which the very notion of "addiction" is often used to describe *and* explain people's drug taking behaviour mirrors in a number of ways the criticisms that she levels at "dependence". Secondly, and perhaps more disturbing, it can be argued that key parts of the addiction literature reveal similar tautological reasoning. For example, examination of sections of certain internationally respected texts that deal with substance-related disorders reveals a number of examples of definition as explanation similar to that which she highlights. This is a cause for anxiety, given the international importance of such works as arbiters on matters of diagnostic criteria. Furthermore, certain of these texts come perilously close to creating some of the kinds of misunderstandings explained in the earlier sections of this chapter.

Definitions of Substance Abuse and Substance Dependence

In the following paragraphs, a number of criticisms are put forward, using examples taken from various sources but making substantial reference to *DSM IV* (A.P.A. 1994). This is not because any of these sources is uniquely flawed, nor is the intention to cast doubt of whatever nature on those who work to compile and update these invaluable documents. The reader is reminded that the main theme of this book is the functionality of drug discourses, whatever their source. *DSM IV* is arguably the most influential and widely respected body of diagnostic knowledge on mental disorders extant. The aim in choosing it is simply to show that, even at the highest and most respected level, discussions of the criteria for addiction struggle with the problems inherent in the addiction concept; and that functionality can be found even in such a body of scientific writing. If evidence of that struggle can be found at this level, small wonder that less erudite sources struggle less successfully.

Under the general chapter heading Substance-Related Disorders, (page 175) *DSM IV* specifies in some detail the criteria for Substance Dependence and Substance Abuse. A number of ambiguous or inadequately-defined words appear frequently in these specifications, and it is the intention next to discuss three of these ("significant"; "maladaptive"; "compulsive") as an illustration of the way in which our notions about substance use problems are shaped and manipulated by the language used to describe them.

Significant. Substance dependence is said to occur when "the individual continues use of the substance despite significant substance-related problems" (page 176). These problems are subsequently listed in tabular form on page 181, and give prominence to cognitive, behavioural and physiological symptoms including tolerance, withdrawal, escalation in the amounts used, and continuing to use despite being aware of adverse consequences ("the substance use is continued despite knowledge of having a persistent or recurrent physical or psychological problem that is likely to have been caused or exacerbated by the substance"). However, the word "significant" (e.g. *as in* significant substance related problem; clinically significant impairment; etc.) is undefined; unless the definition is taken to be implicit in the list of criteria which follow. Semantically, however, the reader is entitled to deduce that there must consequently also be categories of *non-significant* substance related problems, and patterns of substance related clinically *non-significant* impairment or distress which are not discussed; otherwise, the word has no discriminatory value and is merely a label. Consequently, despite the appearance of precision, the issue as to whether a particular problem is "significant" or not remains far from clear.

With respect to the criteria for Substance Abuse, a definition is offered in terms of "a maladaptive pattern of substance use manifested by recurrent and significant adverse consequences".

Interestingly, in the table of Criteria for Substance Abuse (pages 182-183) the prologue is basically the same as that for Substance Dependence, and makes similar reference to clinically significant distress and impairment. "Significant" is again undefined. The criteria listed, however, have far more to do with the failure to fulfil role requirements or duties than do the criteria for dependence. They include "expulsions from school" as a criterion for substance abuse. One might be forgiven for gently pointing out that in the UK at least, many private schools operate a somewhat totalitarian policy on things like cannabis and other so-called soft drugs, with automatic expulsion for offenders, whilst other schools operate a more relaxed and perhaps less destructive policy. According to *DSM IV*, expulsion is a criterion for abuse, so the precise clinical status of one's hash smoking activities rests on the type of drug policy implemented by the school, rather than the nature of the habit itself.

It is possible to argue that the above comments are somewhat nit-picking. After all, clinical judgement is essential for the smooth running of any type of service, and the word "significant" merely allows for such judgement to impinge on the situation. That much is conceded. Nonetheless, the use of the word gives an aura of scientific precision (as in "statistically significant") to what is basically a pragmatic and "seat of the pants" exercise.

Maladaptive. However, there are more important aspects of *DSM IV* to discuss. Both sets of criteria for Dependence and Abuse refer to patterns of substance use which are "maladaptive" with the word maladaptive now requiring definition. The word is employed again in a similar context on page 182, where "a maladaptive pattern of substance use" is seen as being the essential feature of substance abuse. This use of the term "maladaptive" is problematic. Its use clearly implies the existence of a set of similar drug use behaviours which are "adaptive", since otherwise the term has no discriminatory power or meaning; but once again no guidance is forthcoming about how to make this discrimination. Consequently, in the absence of such guidance, one might be forgiven for harbouring the suspicion that the word is being used not in any precise semantic way (i.e. as a term which enables some sort of principled differentiation to be made) but is merely included to display some disapproval, and that ALL recreational drug use might be seen as maladaptive by the producers of *DSM IV*. Notwithstanding this speculation, the undefined nature of "maladaptive" means that this also is open to personal interpretation.

Whilst one might see the justification for allowing clinicians to make judgements about what is, or is not, clinically significant, one might be less sanguine about allowing them the same leeway to judge what is "adaptive". According to the Oxford Dictionary (1990), to "adapt" means amongst other things, to become adjusted to new conditions, and to make suitable for a purpose. Does the word "maladaptive" within *DSM IV* then imply, for example, that ecstasy (MDMA) use at a rave represents a failure to adjust to new conditions? That ecstasy is not suitable for its purpose? Or is it perhaps *DSM IV* which is failing to adjust to new conditions (i.e. a world in which a sizeable proportion of perfectly normal teenagers use drugs recreationally) and it is the very purpose itself which is disapproved of? In short, are the preconceptions in *DSM IV* about what are suitable purposes for a drug separated from the phenomenon itself by gulfs of professional class that are too wide to bridge?

Within the scientific literature, the word "adaptive" has also come to have specific connotations within the theory of evolution and the process of natural selection. From a scientific (i.e. evolutionary) perspective, what justification is there for labelling the behaviour as maladaptive? Do clinicians have the capacity to see into the future, and divine the impact of, say, cannabis smoking on the ultimate survival of the human race? And if so, what about other things? In terms of environmental damage, and the degrading of the biosphere, the habit of driving about in cars has much to answer for. Yet there is little rush on the part of clinicians to label car driving as "maladaptive", despite the fact that the activity appears to merit the use of the word rather better than does the habit of getting out of one's brains at a dance. At the very least, it must be plain that car driving and other acts of global pollution represent a threat at the species level which taking ecstasy at a rave does not.

Finally on this topic, the ways in which species are believed to adapt to new or changing conditions is through natural selection. Individual species members which do not have the genetic capacity to adapt die out, whilst others survive, the result being a gene pool that offers a basis for characteristics and behaviours better suited to the environmental pressures operating. The use of the word "maladaptive" in the present context implies that it is known that the opposite of this process is taking place when people indulge in particular patterns of drug use; that the essential feature of such drug use is that it is part of a localised process of extinction.

Such knowledge, however, is simply not granted to any member of the human race and would be tantamount to prophesy. And if, as may well be the case, the world in the 21st century will be one in which illicit drug use is widespread, then it is at least plausible that current drug use is part of an *adaptive* process (in terms of natural selection) with non-use possibly even being maladaptive (in the sense of failing to adapt to new conditions).

Thus, whilst one might wholeheartedly endorse the clinician's right to judge on matters of clinical significance, his/her ability to judge whether a behaviour is adaptive or maladaptive appears therefore to be more speculative. The fundamental problem for the clinician is, however, that in order to apply the criteria for either dependence or abuse he/she has to take the preliminary step of identifying a particular behaviour as maladaptive in the first place. If it is not maladaptive, then the criteria by implication do not apply. But *DSM IV* is silent on the issue of how to do that, other than by offering a McMurran-type tautology, within which there is no external referent for defining "maladaptive". A maladaptive pattern is manifested in the criteria, and the criteria define maladaptive. In such a case, where there is no external referent or definition, the word is linguistically redundant in any explanatory sense. One could equally well use an algebraic term such as `x' to represent such a cluster since in the circumstances this would have the same (lack of) explanatory power.

Unfortunately, because non-specialist people may be familiar with the terms adaptive and maladaptive, in the sense that they possess assumptions about what the terms mean, they may well assume that their use in prominent and high-status manuals derives from an *independent* knowledge base, rather than by *definition*. In fact, this is not the case. It is suggested instead that terms of this type creep into our texts because of the need for covertly pejorative descriptors; by the side of which the fact that they are themselves defined in terms of the sets of criteria they have been chosen to describe (i.e. in terms of a circularity) seems more or less irrelevant. After all, some disapproval has to be registered somehow. However, if the above argument holds any water, substituting an algebraic label such as 'x' would not, after all, fit the bill. Substituting 'x' would be unsatisfactory, because it would lack the lay connotations that "adaptive" and "maladaptive", in a purely rhetorical sense, evoke.

In order for the above case to have merit, it is not necessary to attribute conscious bad motives or intentions to anyone. It is based merely on a theory of the way language works; i.e. it is functional and performative. One's choice of words is determined by the ends they are intended to serve; and this is as true for scientists as for anyone else. The central theme of this book is the characteristic ways in which drug users employ this ubiquitous process, but it applies to everyone. The danger is that particular subgroups may lay claim to be exempt; for example that science is the disinterested search after truth. The greatest danger is to deny, or claim exception from, such discursive processes; or to believe that science is so exempt.

Compulsive. Perhaps the word "compulsive" can lay claim to being the most abused word in the addiction literature. The word "compulsive" derives from the verb to compel, and means "compelling", or "to bring about by force" (Concise Oxford Dictionary, 1990); and the definition of "compulsive" itself includes "acting from compulsion against one's conscious wishes". At the present time there is great value attached to "compulsive" explanations for behaviour, as such explanations offer two advantages. Firstly, within a Western system of moral thinking and development, one is absolved from the consequences of actions one has performed; and secondly in certain instances responsibility may be directed elsewhere.

It is very difficult to find clear definitions of the word "compulsive". In a definition of addiction, Jaffe (1975) offers the following:

> "... a behavioural pattern of compulsive drug use, characterised by overwhelming involvement with the use of drug, the securing of its supply, and a high tendency to relapse after withdrawal..."

Addiction is here defined in terms of a compulsive pattern of use, with the definition of compulsive giving pride of place to "overwhelming involvement with" the substance. This approach to definition illustrates one of the issues already raised. Addiction is firstly defined in terms of a second entity (compulsive use), and this second entity is then said to be characterised by "overwhelming involvement". However, an overwhelming involvement has nothing in principle to do with compulsion; there is nothing necessarily compulsive about being overwhelmingly involved with something. David Hockney is overwhelmingly involved with painting; Yehudi Menuhin with music; and Mother Theresa with looking after the poor in Calcutta. This definition of compulsion comes close therefore to an abuse of the native language of the type described earlier, because at the end of the day the final level of definition is lacking completely in any sense of compulsion. On what basis can we justify the ascription "compulsive" to an act simply because the person is "overwhelmingly involved" in it? (it is proposed to set to one side the fact that "overwhelmingly" is itself yet another undefined term/value judgement). To say than a particular behaviour in which a person is overwhelmingly involved is "compulsive" is therefore to use the term in an arbitrary way, rather like Humpty Dumpty in *Alice Through the Looking Glass* (*"When I use a word, it means just what I choose it to mean – neither more nor less".* Carrol, L., 1896)

Another example may be taken from Cox *et al.*(1983, page 31);

> "Psychological dependence is ordinarily manifested in the form of compulsive drug-taking habits, but the frequency and pattern of habit can differ considerably from one individual to another."

Once again, in answer to the question, "How do I recognise psychological dependence?" we receive in effect the answer "First look for some compulsive drug taking". But there is no advice on how to discriminate between compulsive and non-compulsive behaviours. Moreover, the situation is complicated by the fact that although "compulsive" implies "overwhelming involvement" (see above), we have to bear in mind that the habit can differ fundamentally between individuals. That is, "overwhelming" is not strictly quantitative in terms of the above definition. One person's drug use may be overwhelming, and hence compulsive, at levels of use which are lower and less frequent than another person's, whose use is heavier and more frequent, but not overwhelming and hence non-compulsive. It must be plain that "compulsive" in this context actually has no operational definition. Once again we must conclude that the choice of this word to describe drug use derives in no sense from a clear scientific definition, but from the need to ensure that drug use continues to be viewed in a particular light by a lay audience who make assumptions about what lies behind the use of the word; i.e. that science has "proved" that drug use is compulsive.

There are broader issues at stake here. There have apparently been recent cases in the USA where violent criminal offenders have attempted to claim a retrial in the light of the evidence for a genetic basis for violent assaultive crime. If this evidence is true, it is reasoned, then those concerned were in some sense compelled to commit the crimes by their genetic constitutions and thus cannot be held responsible (and hence guilty) since their actions were forced by circumstances beyond their control. In legal terms, it is suggested, they could not have behaved otherwise. This will perhaps strike many, if not most readers, as both absurd and outrageous, a corruption of what may be inferred about social behaviour from the study of genetics. The fact that some situation or circumstance is associated with a more frequent manifestation of a certain form of behaviour cannot become the occasion for assuming that such behaviour is thus inevitable or "compelled" and that therefore no individual personal responsibility is involved (for example, there is evidence for a genetic basis to musicality; this does not mean that everyone possessing this trait is compelled to be a musician, and could not do otherwise). There would surely be ethical objections at a societal level if such evidence were used on a broad scale to mitigate antisocial criminal acts by individuals.

However, not all examples evoke such a clear social reaction. Recent class actions by smokers against the tobacco manufacturers are probably more socially acceptable, and so the idea that mechanism simply replaces decision-making finds more support in this area. One of the key issues here is the suggestion that smokers are forced to smoke by the nicotine in tobacco (Surgeon General's Report, 1988). The argument is likely to be, once again, that they could not have behaved otherwise. Whilst the relative risk factors for active smoking suggest convincingly that the habit is an important risk factor in certain illnesses, the notion that people who smoke in the face of well-known health risks are "compelled" to do so, and cannot act otherwise, is a very different issue.

Clearly, the idea of *compulsive behaviour* can be used to support a number of claims, both popular and unpopular, and our reaction seems to have more to do with how we feel about the issue in question (we feel sympathy for smokers, but not for violent criminals) and less with the underlying logic of the proposition. Meanwhile, the social usefulness of compulsive explanations as removers of individual responsibility suggests that they will become more rather than less popular, especially where scientists continue to offer mechanistic explanations as the only "real" bases of behaviour. Perhaps we may look forward to some time not too far distant when, somewhat bizarrely, committed drinkers will sue the landlord of their "local", heroin and cocaine "addicts" will sue their local drug dealers, and "shopaholics" will sue their local supermarkets, over the negative consequences of their chosen habits, on the grounds that they could not have behaved otherwise.

The socially-mandated use of compulsive explanations is not limited to the addiction arena. One of the more popular "compulsive" explanations is "peer group pressure", especially valued by parents when their offspring perpetrate some delinquency. Whilst text-book definitions of the phenomenon are often complex, reflexive and highly differentiated, and view the process as a reciprocal system of *social influence,* the term "peer group pressure" has now taken on a life and function of its own. That life derives from a lay understanding that "peer group pressure" means somebody did something because they were pressurised (compelled) by their peers; and this misperception is reinforced by health education messages in the media portraying innocent victims being pressured into drug use by wicked peers who use coercion and threats. Parents understand this message very well indeed and appreciate its usefulness. It means that Samantha had no responsibility (was not to blame) for smoking hash in the playground. Thankfully, she is after all a good girl who was forced to do it against her will by others who were bad, and all she needs is some "Just Say No" counselling (it remains a mystery why one so seldom meets the parents of the "bad" ones; for the most part, all one encounters are parents of the innocent victims of other children's negative peer group pressure). Fortunately, there are more subtle accounts of this phenomenon which give due consideration to peer preference, mutual influence, and individual motives (Coggans & McKeller, 1994).

Furthermore, in 1992 the author was involved in research into HIV/AIDS and drug use in a number of European prisons (Shewan, Davies, & Henderson, 1992), and underwent a salutory learning experience. In one European capital, an interview on the subject of drug use in prison was carried out with a woman who had been involved in certain terrorist activities as a member of the Red Brigade, and who had recently been released from prison. On first entering the prison, she had been taken into a cell by a group of other women, a knife had been held to her throat, and she was told that unless she agreed to have sex as required they would kill her. Peer group pressure indeed! (a colleague remarked, "Now that's what *I* call peer group pressure."). Taking the above example, we can thus justifiably take the view that the sexual activities in which she was involved were "compelled". In this instance we agree with McMurran therefore; we can *see* the source of compulsion only too clearly. However, whilst agreeing that the activity was "compelled", to describe it as "compulsive sex" seemed somehow inappropriate. It slowly dawned that, in terms of general understandings, the adjective "compulsive" has taken on an existence and meaning which is now largely independent of the verb "to compel", to the extent that "compulsive" is largely reserved for phenomena where there are in fact *no* easily observable and external sources which can be seen to compel. Thus someone forced to commit a crime at gunpoint would not be called a compulsive thief; someone forced to gamble at gunpoint would not be called a compulsive gambler. The way the word "compulsive" is actually used, therefore, is in a highly idiosyncratic way to describe patterns of frequent and regular behaviour for which no external compelling agent is in fact visible. That is, for situations where somebody does something "bad" over and over again, for no obvious reason. In such circumstances, "compulsion" is an inference, or rather an un-warranted assumption about the presence of inner forces that compel, and not a behavioural observation. It is based on nothing more than the pre-scientific assumption that no "normal" person would do such a thing, and that therefore the action must be "compelled" by something we cannot see.

Consequently, a final issue is raised concerning the unconscious egocentrism (in the sense of being unable to take another person's viewpoint) that characterises some of the writing on drug problems. For example, according to *DSM IV* (page 179) a key issue in recognising compulsive use is not the existence of the problem itself, but the failure of the individual to desist in the face of clear evidence that the behaviour is causing difficulties. ("The key issue in evaluating this criterion is not the existence of the problem, but rather the individual's failure to abstain from using the substance despite having evidence of the difficulty it is causing.") Implicit in this statement is a difficulty on the part of the authors in contemplating or acknowledging a possible rational basis for repeated actions that have foreseeable negative consequences. From such a viewpoint, the only framework that can be brought to bear is one of compulsion and pathology; because the key to compulsion, in clinical terms, is the fact that a person keeps on doing something despite negative outcomes that *someone else thinks would cause any "normal" person to desist*. It is almost as if the authors' own fear and timorousness in the face of negative behavioural outcomes is assumed to be "normal" and to constitute a benchmark against which others, from completely different walks of life, may be impartially judged. Clearly, such a viewpoint is only one of several different viewpoints it is possible to take towards drug use.

The key assumption by the person offering the definition is that his or her views on the topic are prototypical; and that consequently, no normal person could possibly like or enjoy the activity in the circumstances. Consequently, they must be in the grip of an invisible compulsion. Simple ideas of the type that the positive aspects of the behaviour may be more prized by the individual than the negative aspects are feared, appear to have no place in this argument. Neither do positive qualities such as doggedness, perseverance, stoicism, and single mindedness. In typical contentious style, Saunders (1995) writes *"Drug induced `highs' are as worthy, noble, desirable, problematic, bad, indifferent and moral, as the so-called `natural highs'. The use of mescaline, magic mushrooms or morphine is as meritorious as mountaineering, motor-car racing and muscle-building."* We do not have to agree with the specifics to take the point that there has to be some empirical basis for the *a priori* assumption that an activity, whatever its nature, is simply and straightforwardly bad or abnormal, within any discourse purporting to be scientific. In the absence of such, we are left with a primarily moral, rather than a scientific, judgement.*

But what about people who continue with a certain type of behaviour despite clear evidence of damaging consequences?

In recent times, some of the most intensely readable and expressive writings on the subject of mountaineering have been produced by the climber Joe Simpson. Simpson suffered catastrophic fracture of the leg in an incident made famous by the book Touching the Void, in which he recounts his fall of some thousands of feet from Siula Grande in South America, where he ended up in the crevasse at the foot of the mountain. A few years later he sustained similar injuries to his other leg in a fall from the East face of Pachermo. Both injuries required repeated surgery and recovery periods of some years. For long periods Simpson had the most severe problems with simply walking, and still experiences difficulty. Yet before he was fully recovered, he was climbing again. In his

---

*This is not an argument against the making of moral judgements. It is an argument against expressing moral judgements in such a way that they appear to be of scientific origin, and therefore a 'superior' form of truth.

most recent book (*This Game of Ghosts, 1994*) a photograph shows Simpson *climbing on crutches*, at a height of 20,000 feet on Pumori. In that book Simpson tells of these events, and also discusses poignantly the deaths of a number of colleagues in climbing accidents of the most spectacular and heartbreaking nature. Simpson thus continued to climb despite clear and unambiguous knowledge of serious negative consequences both for himself and for other close friends.

One could therefore describe his behaviour as maladaptive and compulsive, and make out a strong case that he has suffered "significant impairment" (according to Simpson himself, he now has a choice of which leg to limp with), with the implication that his behaviour is pathological. Or one could describe it as single minded, spirited and incredibly courageous. The choice of terminology would not depend on "scientific fact", but on how one felt about climbing; and perhaps upon whether one had any positive personal experience or understanding of the magical sense of remoteness, fear and fulfilment to be found from exploring high and dangerous places. In the absence of such experience or understanding, (and particularly if the mere *prospect* of clinging to a vertical ice wall by the point of an axe in a freezing blizzard arouses in one nothing but an avoidance reaction, and a feeling that such behaviour cannot possibly be *sensible* if no spark in the soul says "I want to know what that feels like; to view that terrible vista; to feel that particular dreadful fear") one would probably use the terms maladaptive and compulsive to describe Simpson's behaviour.

However, in the absence of operational definition the words are merely terms of covert denigration deriving from a lack of empathy and comprehension; terms of abuse applied to the activities of one group by another group which has no comprehension or phenomenological rapprochement with the activity in question. An alternative description would be that Joe Simpson is dedicated, single minded, committed to climbing, and that his writings on the subject enrich our literary heritage in general, and our understanding of the desire to climb in particular. To dismiss his achievements as mere "compulsive climbing" because of their palpable negative consequences (the forced manifestations of a pathology) would be to rob them of their humanity and their virtue. It is difficult to find anything pleasing about types of explanation that have such a property of reducing human action to the status of the mere outcomes of highly localised physical laws, thereby robbing human behaviour of its contextual, social and motivational significance.

Definition as rhetoric

The above paragraphs seek to make out the case that the use of a number of terms which are central to the addiction field is better understood as a series of rhetorical acts than as the reporting of a series of scientific "truths". The purpose of these rhetorical acts is to appeal to lay understandings of the terms employed. On the basis of those understandings the public, the media, politicians and others assume there is *shared* understanding deriving from a body of scientific facts. However, such a body of facts is sometimes based on highly circumscribed and esoteric definitions which may be far removed from lay understandings, and in some cases such a body of facts may not exist at all. For example, a lay understanding presumes that "science" has "proved" the compulsive and maladaptive nature of drug use in terms of an independent body of knowledge, when in fact careful reading shows that no such knowledge exists. In its place, we have the selection of pejorative terms which are defined by the phenomena they are used to summarise. Therefore, lacking operational definition, they provide no principled basis for differentiation; and being defined in terms of a circularity they have no explanatory power. In such cases, functional discourse, that is language designed to have a particular effect on the reader rather than to describe "truth", has replaced what is commonly understood by "scientific writing".

In the following chapters, increasing reference will be made to the rhetorical and functional nature of the things that drug users say about their habit. It is the hope that the present chapter will dispel any assumption that such functional rhetoric is confined only to those who actually use and misuse the substances in question. Functional acts of speech are, as we have seen, easy to find on both sides of the addiction fence, characterising not merely the utterances of many drug users, but also the writings of many whose task is to study, and/or ameliorate, the problems caused by the unwise or doggedly determined use of drugs.

4

The Status of
Verbal Report

The arguments presented in the previous chapters can be refuted, it may be argued, by the simple expedient of heeding the verbal reports of drug users themselves. McMurran (*op. cit.*) for example certainly appears to imply that verbal reports of personal experience can be taken as veridical descripters of, and reliable substitutes for observations of, things themselves or people's experience of things ("…. withdrawal, compulsion and diminished control are all clinically observed phenomena. That is, certain people can be seen to experience them, *or can tell you that they have these experiences…*" p. 75, my italics). Clients' verbal reports of their own experience are thus of equal epistemological status to clinicians' observations of behaviour and experience.* Ignoring for the time being the problem of whether experience and reality occupy the same or different worlds, we totally accept the idea that drug users can tell you whether their drug use is compulsive or not, whether they are addicted or not, whether they can stop or not, whether they are in the grip of a biological/pharmacological force which is irresistible or not, and so forth. It is argued here, however, that such statements are primarily functional and symbolic. Least of all can such statements be taken as objective insights by drug users into the functioning of their own bodies, since it is

---

*There appears to be an attempt here to circumvent the problem of whether experience is "real", in the sense that McMurran implies on the one hand that experience parallels reality ["That is…" etc] whilst leaving the door open for the possibility that it might not. Whatever the case, the idea that either compulsion to use drugs, or the experience of compulsion to use drugs, are things that can be directly observed, as opposed to merely inferred, is a contentious issue.

argued that it is in principle not possible for people to have access to such information about themselves. However, this does not prevent them from providing functional answers which help to make sense of their situation when such a question is asked. The remainder of this text now seeks to provide evidence in support of these conclusions.

From a philosophical standpoint, the nature of language is problematic and many learned texts have been written on the subject. One of the central problems is how to answer the question "What are people doing when they use language?" The scope of this question is vast, and too broad to be covered adequately within this text whose specific remit is to shed light on the nature of addiction. However, one of the central debates is in fact highly germane. Namely, can people use language to describe the *processes* by means of which their brains work? This seemingly obvious question is in fact rather complex, and there is no clear answer. However, one possible answer is "Yes they can, because introspection allows people direct access to their own processes of thought, and therefore they can tell us about them". On the other hand, and perhaps more cogently (because it requires fewer non-parsimonious assumptions) it is possible to argue "No they cannot, because the introspections and the verbal reports about them are themselves the *products* of the processes involved, not the processes themselves".

These arguments were brought together in a seminal paper by Nisbett and Wilson (1977) entitled "Telling more than we can know: verbal reports on mental process". Nisbett and Wilson argued that verbal reports about mental processes (e.g. why people decide to do certain things and not others) were not what they seemed to be semantically. Reports of mental processes were *not* equivalent to reports of external events, the only differences being that this time the observation was directed inward rather than towards the external world. Such internal observation, they argued, was probably not possible. Consequently, the derivation and nature of the reports obtained had to be sought elsewhere in terms of demand characteristics of experiments, making sense of situations, implicit previously learned causal theories and other factors. Subsequently, the Nisbett and Wilson paper was heavily criticised, but it retains much of its credibility and raises issues which have not all been satisfactorily resolved.

Perhaps one of the reasons that Nisbett and Wilson's paper came under so much fire was that it threatened the very basis of a number of social research methods geared to the notion that people's verbal utterances about their motives, intentions, attitudes, beliefs and so forth described something going on inside their heads. In contrast, they were obliquely suggesting that such verbal reports derived primarily from the very tasks the psychologists (or whoever) had themselves devised and perhaps had little relevance beyond that context; or that they were selections from a set of socially learned "stories" or explanatory discourses which seemed appropriate or sensible-to-say in a certain experimental setting but whose aetiology was very different from that which was assumed. In the present context, for example, it is interesting to ask the question, "How would a person know that they were addicted?" Would this come about through the privileged self-observation of the state of their meso-acumbens; or by means of publicly observing, along with everyone else, that they were using drugs with great regularity, an observation which required some justification? (Bem, 1972)

Whatever the truth of the matter, it is certainly the case that either of two positions is tenable on this issue. On the one hand, people's verbal reports might give a true account of processes taking place in their heads (a basically dualist perspective that leaves unanswered the questions "Who is the reporter of the events, and who the participant in those processes? And can one person be both?"); or on the other hand, people's verbal reports might be the consequences of processes taking place, not the processes themselves.

It is paradoxical that many psychologists like to take bits from both these philosophies and try to weave them into a coherent picture despite their basic incompatibility. The rigour and parsimony employed in the study of behaviour appears to be routinely abandoned where verbal behaviour is concerned. Language, it appears, is treated as a special case.

One of the most influential paradigms within psychology has been, and still is in many quarters, the body of theory and research method subsumed under the general title of "Behaviourism". Amongst a glittering array of names who have espoused this doctrine in a variety of forms, perhaps the name of B.F. Skinner is best known. Skinner is perhaps most famous for his contributions to the theory and practice of operant conditioning, based on the notion that behaviour is reinforced by contingent events in the environment. The Skinner box, with its lever, which the occupant (usually a rat or a pigeon) is induced to push in return for reinforcement, represents the archetypal operant conditioning procedure. The probability of the behaviour occurring is influenced by the reinforcement offered and the system (schedule) underlying the occurrence of the reward. From such humble beginnings Skinner offered plans for entire societies in which the environment was planned in such a way as to reinforce positive and sociable behaviours, including altruism and tolerance for delayed gratification (Skinner, B.F., 1938; 1948; 1978).

Whilst there are serious conceptual problems with Skinner's idea (see chapter 3 in Davies 1992 *op. cit.*) and the Utopia seems as far away as ever, the actual techniques are still widely used for investigations of the behaviour of unfortunate animals in somewhat artificial environments and also for a more restricted set of experimental studies of human action in a variety of settings. Less well known, perhaps, are Skinner's thoughts on how his system would apply to language, a set of ideas put forward in the book *Verbal Behaviour* (Skinner, 1957). Central to Skinner's ideas about language is the notion that the principles of reinforcement which he adduces to explain other behaviours also explain language. People say things because their "language behaviour" is reinforced by environmental contingencies. The well-springs of language are thus the same as the well-springs of any other kind of behaviour (this is perhaps the central point of disagreement between Skinner and Chomsky) and language enjoys no privileged position in that respect within Skinner's system. The point being made here is not whether Skinner's system is "right" or "true" but merely whether it is internally consistent; and with respect to the position "language behaviour" occupies within that system in relation to other behaviours, one would have to conclude that it was in fact consistent. No case is made within the theory that language behaviour is somehow "special", that its roots lie anywhere other than in environmental contingencies of reinforcement, nor that it gives any special route of access to processes or entities in the brain (mind), domains and capabilities which are specifically excluded (Skinner 1974, chapters 2 and 13). Language allows no special access to privileged types of information; it can only illustrate within a particular area of action the same laws of reinforcement that are revealed by acts such as kicking a football, pressing a lever, or eating a sandwich.

It is paradoxical therefore to find hard-nosed and behaviouristically oriented scientists using verbal reports from subjects as independent variables on the basis of which to group or classify subjects involved in experiments investigating (for example) the reinforcing effects of drugs. And equally strange that reflexive psychologists, discourse theorists, social constructionists or other advocates of soft-nosed or "unscientific" science should be the ones to point out that such procedures are "unscientific". If one sees oneself as operating within a behaviouristic operant conditioning paradigm, then the principles of that type of psychology ought to apply as much to verbal behaviour as to any other type of behaviour or else the whole Skinnerian edifice starts to wobble. The assumption that Skinnerian principles apply to all behaviours except language behaviours would be one such wobble-inducing assumption; if it doesn't apply to language, then maybe it doesn't apply to other things as well. It would therefore not be theoretically coherent to (for example) examine the effects of different types of schedules of drug reinforcement on "craving", if the measure of craving consisted of some verbal reports (questionnaire answers, ticks on a craving scale, self-reports or whatever) obtained from subjects in response to a request from the experimenter to provide such data. Within that research paradigm, the reasons for the very verbal reports themselves would have to be sought in the environment, and probably the immediate environment of the experiment where they are sometimes not too difficult to find (Rosenthal, 1966). The reports of craving cannot be taken as some kind of verbally isomorphic representation of a craving entity in the head, taken from some special domain of behaviour to which reinforcement principles do not apply, since such is not permissable within the overall philosophy of the experiment. In other words, one cannot take reports of craving to be unreinforced verbal representations of internal entities or states without shedding doubt on the entire "operant" theory itself. If verbal behaviour has the capacity to be independent of reinforcement contingencies, so might other forms of behaviour.

It is not necessary to agree wholeheartedly with Skinner's view of language, which is probably misconceived, nor indeed with his views of anything else, in order to encounter the serious problems to which this line of argument gives rise. It is only necessary to accept that acts of speech are motivated or "functional". If we can agree that such is the case (i.e. that speech acts are motivated; that people say things for reasons, rather than simply retrieving "facts" from a memory store after the fashion of a computer; that people edit and manipulate what they say according to circumstances) then certain things follow. First and foremost, (and leaving aside the previous debate about whether it is in fact possible for people to report on their own mental processes *at all*) acceptance of the fact that verbal reports are *even sometimes* motivated means that they can *never* constitute satisfactory "scientific" data in terms of their own semantic content. Just as with Popper's view of science, multiple replications can never "prove" a theory whilst a single failure to replicate can refute it, so with verbal behaviour. If verbal reports can even sometimes be motivated acts rather than acts of veridical reporting, there always exists the possibility that in the specific case that is what they were (i.e. motivated acts). Consequently, they can never be used in terms of their surface meaning to serve as "scientific data".

If, as is more probably the case, verbal reports are almost always motivated, and there is no such thing as an unmotivated discursive act then the problem is fundamental rather than nit-picking.

The qualitative/quantitative debate

To argue that verbal reports can never serve as "scientific" data in terms of their semantics is not to argue that such data are therefore "useless". Qualitative use of such data sheds light (arguably) on how people perceive various situations; and their comments certainly serve to put some flesh and colour on the bones of many an otherwise dry research report. But is it "scientific"? And does it matter if it isn't? At the time of writing, the qualitative/ quantitative debate is in full swing in a number of areas, including addiction; the journal *Addiction* (1995) recently carried a lead article by McKegany (1995) followed by a number of commentaries in the same, and subsequent issues. Basically, the argument centres around whether quantitative and qualitative methods are complementary, or whether they are philosophically incompatible. A recent editorial in *Health Education Research* (Davies, 1996) argues for the second of these alternative positions and suggests the need for an alternative conception of verbal report that brings both qualitative and quantitative data into the same philosophical fold.

A number of excellent texts on the use of qualitative data appear in the literature (e.g. Miles & Hubermann 1984; Silverman, 1985) and it is not proposed to reiterate the main points here. It remains to be said, however, that qualitative data are sometimes used in an unprincipled manner (in the sense that there is no underlying set of logical and procedural principles which others could follow in order to arrive necessarily at a similar conclusion) with selected extracts being singled out for inclusion in a final report primarily because they illustrate the points the author already wishes to make. Such usage does not even comply with the flawed requirements of science as discussed earlier; not in itself a problem, unless one claims or implies that it does. (e.g. see Potter and Wetherell's (*op. cit.*) discussion of a study of football violence by Marsh *et al.* in 1978. They demonstrate that the researchers treat different parts of the data obtained from the soccer fans in different ways, treating some utterances as merely rhetorical and others as genuine or true. The basis for this distinction appears to be personal belief, and Potter and Wetherell conclude that there are "damaging inconsistencies in the way discourse is interpreted in this study" (pp. 61-62).)

However, the qualitative route is not the only alternative available. It is unfortunate that in the existing literature qualitative and quantitative methods are seen as in some sense opposites, with alternative philosophical underpinnings. However, it is possible to argue that any method relying on verbal report, whether this is justified in terms of a quantitative or a qualitative ideology, basically deals with the same raw material. It is most unlikely that subjects in a qualitative study have any clear sense that the quality of their thoughts has just been assessed; nor that those in a quantitative study have any sense that their mental processes have just been "measured" in the way that one might be measured for a suit. From the point of view of the subject, one merely responds in an acquiescent way to the demands made by the psychologist, on the assumption that he/she presumably knows what they are doing when eliciting answers to questions in one way rather than another.

The raw material is the same; it merely comes out differently as a consequence of the differing cueing strategies (elicitation procedures) chosen by the experimenter. From such a viewpoint, it is possible to see reports as being sensitive to the methods used by the experimenter; and these methods as having the effect of setting or altering the subjects' criterion for offering one type of verbal report rather than another. Finally, the choice of method adopted by the experimenter may also be seen as an indicant of *the experimenter's* own motivation, since choice of method influences the nature of the data obtained, and, by and large, experimenters will choose methods which offer the best chance of confirming an hypothesis or theory, rather than the opposite.

From such a viewpoint, motivated verbal reports are obtained by motivated methods which offer greater or lesser opportunities for certain kinds of reportage, or more or less degrees of freedom in terms of the response formats offered. There is nothing in principle that guarantees "truer" responses, or "more accurate" responses, regardless of which method is chosen; and consequently neither is one particularly qualitative whilst the other is especially quantitative. What exists is a range of motivated verbal reports cued with greater or lesser degrees of specificity by a researcher with particular aims (if not outcomes) in mind; and a range of intrinsic (to the experiment) and extrinsic (societal) factors which affect the subject's criterion for saying one thing rather than something else. There is no basis for saying either that, on the one hand, the so called quantitative reports must in principle reflect the status of entities or processes in the brain (mind), nor for asserting that so called qualitative reports accurately reflect individual perceptions or experiences. Since verbal reports can be (are?) motivated and selective accounts rather than computer-like retrieval from storage, the data obtained in any given case can never be treated as veridical. The best that can ever be said is that they might be.

In these circumstances, it might be argued that the correct line of enquiry for the psychologist is to investigate the relationship between variability in intrinsic and extrinsic (methodological and contextual) factors and subsequent differences (variability) in any verbal reports obtained. This requires no assumptions to be made about the truthfulness or otherwise of particular verbal acts, but by locating particular types of verbal act within certain contexts, the *function* of that act is revealed. At the end of the day, the psychologist may thus say, with appropriate caution, "I know why that person said that thing". And that may strike the reader as a quest entirely appropriate for a psychologist to undertake, more appropriate in fact than the mundane description of who says what, unaccompanied by any theoretical perspective on the functional and contextual (i.e. motivated) nature of the data obtained.

The lesson from classical psychophysics

The joint assertions that (a) the truthfulness of a verbal statement can never be assumed, and (b) the nature of verbal reports obtained in research studies depends on the methods used by the researcher to produce them, appear to cause dismay in some circles, probably because of their implications for research projects that assume the veridical nature of verbal reports about the workings of the mind. Any such dismay is however somewhat misplaced. Even in the arena of physics (the "hardest" of the "hard" sciences) the joint notions that the results of our measurement endeavours depend on where we are when we make them, and that the act of measurement itself affects the thing being measured, are now accepted widely. Thus, at a time when even physicists increasingly encounter problems with specifying the fixed and enduring properties of matter, for psychologists and others to insist that a given method on a single occasion is sufficient to specify the nature of an attitude, belief or whatever seems a little behind the times (Davies, 1966 *op. cit.*).

In terms of a lay understanding and at risk of cutting a number of corners, Einstein's theory is, relatively speaking, analogous to a sort of super context theory. The results obtained from one's measurement endeavours are context dependent; that is "relative" to other things like place, time and speed rather than absolute. On the other hand, Heisenberg's principle is basically a super-experimenter effect; at a sub-molecular level, the act of measurement alters the things being measured (their position or their direction), so our measurements can never be complete or total, and that is why Heisenberg was uncertain. Far from these theories being somewhat abstruse and rarified, the esoteric dominion of the particle accelerator and the electron microscope (and leaving aside the tired old saw that whilst we might be uncertain about sub-atomic particles, we can still rely on billiard balls) from the point of view of the social scientist the world is full of analogous relativity (context) effects and uncertainty principles (experimenter effects). Indeed, these effects are so common and so ubiquitous that we perhaps fail to realise that we confront Einstein-type and Heisenberg-like social phenomena at every twist and turn. So common are they that we fail to see these principles illustrated in our own social research, even though they stare us in the face. In such circumstances, it is hard to understand why alone amongst the sciences psychology still prefers the view of an absolute and certain universe. If physicists can live with ideas of contextuality and reflexivity at the sub-atomic level, it is difficult to see why psychologists cannot do the same when analogous phenomena arguably constitute the very essence of their subject. And given the common notion amongst many "scientific" psychologists that physics provides the scientific model to which psychology should aspire, it would be nice if the model of physics implied was at least contemporary with current thinking in that subject.

But how then is "truth" to be known? If verbal reports are context dependent, and influenced by the experimenter, how is progress to be made? Firstly, it is necessary to say that *if they are,* then there is no choice other than to come to terms with the problems presented. We may not proceed along a particular scientific path simply because it is the only one that suits the methodologies we are familiar with. Secondly, however, help is to hand and the problems may not be as difficult to solve as they seem. There is one classical area of psychology where some of these philosophical dilemmas have been, albeit somewhat inadvertently, addressed. That area is, perhaps surprisingly, psychophysics, a traditional branch of psychology that seeks to establish the range of operation and sensitivities of the sensory modalities (the word "surprisingly" is used because one might have expected the dilemmas of verbal report to be taken on board more fully by those who make the most extensive use of verbal data, rather than by people whose orientation is basically physiological). Because of problems arising within the theory and practice of "classical" psychophysics, the theory of signal detection (S.D.) was developed (Green & Swets, 1966). Paradoxically signal detection theory, one of the most hard-nosed, mathematical and "scientific" branches of human science, has a genuine existential postulate at its core, though the reader will never find it referred to as such in the S.D. literature.

The term "classical psychophysics" encapsulates a body of theory, and a set of precise methods, for establishing absolute and difference thresholds for the human sensory modalities. "Classical" methods could be used to determine what is the lowest level of sound of a particular frequency that a person can hear, or what is the dimmest level of illumination a person can see (both examples of absolute thresholds); or what is the smallest difference in sound level a person can detect between two consecutive tones, or what is the smallest difference in brightness a person can detect between two lights (an example of difference thresholds). Basically, in classical psychophysical studies, subjects are presented with stimuli of varying magnitudes in an extended series of trials, and asked to report on each trial whether or not they perceive it (absolute threshold); or to report which of two stimuli is the louder, brighter, heavier or whatever (difference threshold). The subject indicates by verbal or quasi-verbal report "Yes I see (feel, hear etc.) it" or "No I don't" (absolute threshold); or "The first is louder (brighter, heavier etc.) than the second" or "The two seem to be the same" (difference threshold).

Typically, a classical psychophysical study lasts a long time, and requires many (possibly thousands) of repeated trials. If verbal reports of internal processes were "accurate" and "reliable" of course, a single trial series should do the trick. The subject should give just one account of how his/her internal sensory processes are working and that should establish "the facts". The reasons why so many trials are required is because the verbal reports are inconsistent; or in statistical parlance there is variance in the verbal reports. Thus due to changes in attention, background noise, fatigue, or whatever else, a subject will sometimes fail to report hearing (seeing, feeling or whatever) a stimulus that they reported hearing on a previous trial. Conversely, they will sometimes report perceiving a stimulus that they did not report on a previous trial. Given this variability, the "true threshold" is assumed to emerge over many trials in terms of the average threshold as indicated over the whole series. This is probably a sensible heuristic measure but it is not strictly logical taken at face value and rests on a series of statistical assumptions. No single trial can be said to be accurate, but a true picture is assumed to emerge from the whole series. This is rather like agreeing that within a general survey of alcohol consumption, whilst we can make no claim about the accuracy of any individual set of results, we can nonetheless assume that all these individual reports give a "true picture" of the population consumption when added together. This may or may not be true.

However, classical psychophysics is underlaid by three central assumptions that give a defensible basis to the above procedure (see Scharf, 1975; ch. 2). Three continua are postulated as providing the basis for psychophysical theory, and these are illustrated below in Figure 1.

The first of these continua is the stimulus continuum. The stimulus continuum consists of values of the presented stimulus (sound, light, pressure or whatever) measured in physical units. Values on this continuum are assumed to be fixed and invariant; for example, if the stimulus is a tone of a particular frequency (measured in Hz) and a particular intensity (measured in dB), then the assumption is that the particular tone is identical and invariant

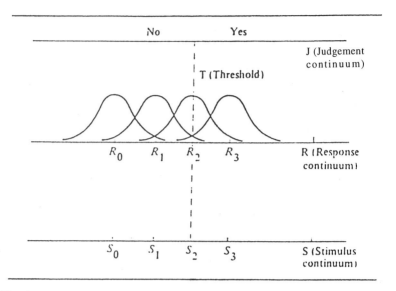

Fig. 1

on all those trials on which it occurs.

The second continuum, the response continuum, is philosophically the most intriguing. The "response" referred to here is not an overt behaviour of the type beloved of Skinnerians, but an internal event taking place inside the organism in "response" to the stimulus. In other words a neurological event triggered by the stimulus. However, unlike the stimulus continuum, the response continuum is assumed to be variable. That is, the magnitude of this internal event may vary from trial to trial even though the stimulus is identical. This is assumed to happen as a consequence of the changing or fluctuating state of the organism due to things such as fatigue, changes in readiness or attention, boredom, distraction, interference or whatever. Consequently, although stimulus values are assumed to be invariant between trials, many trials are nonetheless required so that the more variable events on the internal or response continuum "average out" to a representative mean value.

The third continuum is the judgement continuum. This continuum is in effect the "verbal report" continuum; the one the subject uses to let the experimenter know what he/she heard or saw. Note that the problem of whether people can in fact report about the nature of internal processes raises its head suddenly within this theory; neural responses are triggered or not triggered by stimuli, and subjects just report on whether it happened or not. Within the classical theory of psychophysics, verbal reports are assumed to correlate perfectly ("to correspond perfectly") with events on the response continuum. This, of course, is directly analogous to the social psychologists' assumptions that reports of internal states such as attitudes, intentions, beliefs, norms, values or whatever correspond exactly to some internal state of the organism.

   However, in the area of psychophysics, it has long been accepted that verbal reports on the judgement continuum are not isomorphic with events on the internal response continuum; that in some sense verbal reports have a life of their own, and that the tidy scenario represented by classical psychophysics does not adequately represent the situation. Basically, psychophysicists realised some time ago that, independent of what happens on the response continuum, subjects may have reasons for saying "Yes I hear it" or "No I don't" that derive from other sources altogether. In other words, subjects might have motives for saying one thing rather than the other, and these motives constitute an uncontrolled source of variance in the data. In the parlance of signal detection theory, this is described by saying that the subjects' *criterion* for offering one answer rather than the other might vary at different times and places, and this will affect the verbal decisions they produce.

The theory of signal detection

The problems that confronted the assumptions of classical psychophysics, in the form of evidence that the verbal continuum did not in fact correlate perfectly with the response continuum, was tackled within the theory of signal detection (S.D.) by placing the subject's motives in centre stage. The new variable was termed subject criterion, as indicated above. From this viewpoint, although there were clearly stimuli that people could perceive and stimuli they could not, the idea that there was a "true" or "real" threshold that held true for all situations and circumstances was abandoned. The reasoning behind the abandonment of the idea of "real" or "true" thresholds was partly due to the fact that there could be no such thing as a verbal report that did not derive from a particular criterion position. Consequently, if the criterion changed, so apparently did the threshold value. In the words of Snodgrass (cited from Scharf *op. cit.* ch. 2) "What appears to be a threshold is in fact a response criterion. The only reason the person appears to have a threshold is that he is forced to distinguish between signal and noise" (in this context, "noise" is any background against which a signal is presented).

If we take Snodgrass literally, and transfer the arguments from the measurement of sensory thresholds to the measurement of attitudes, we might thus come up with some formulation like the following:— *"What appears to be an attitude (belief, value, or whatever) is in fact a response criterion. The only reason the person appears to have an attitude (belief etc.) is that he is forced to distinguish between five points on an attitude (or whatever) scale."* Note that the precise analogy being made concerns the requirement of subjects to report about some internal state, and the evidence that verbal report does not correlate perfectly with events on some internal dimension.

The signal detection theorist's answer to this problem was both mathematically complex and conceptually rather elegant and simple. If the subject's motive (criterion) for saying one thing rather than another is uncontrolled, then we will in future design our perception studies so that criterion is controlled. In signal detection experiments, criterion is brought under control basically by introducing new motivational variables into the study, so that subjects' answers can be described under varying conditions of incentive as well as various strengths of signal. A simple way to achieve this is to induce subjects to adopt a range of criterion positions, ranging from lax (under which conditions subjects will report hearing a wide range of signals including ones that are "below threshold") through to strict (under which circumstances subjects will only report perceiving the most obvious signals) and a range of criterion positions in between. And the means of altering the subjects' criterion position can be very simple; we can either offer rewards for any correct detections or HITS (i.e. saying "yes" when a signal is in fact presented) or punishing FALSE POSITIVES (saying "yes" on trials when in fact nothing is presented). Giving or taking away money is one simple way of providing rewards and punishments. Rewarding hits produces a lax criterion; punishing false positives produces a strict criterion; and by manipulating the relative amounts of rewards and punishments a variety of intermediate criterion positions can be obtained.

At the end of the day, the data are summarised in terms of simple graphs or curves (known as ROC curves) which in effect plot subjects' perceptual decisions (verbal responses) about various stimuli over a range of criterion positions. Consequently, any questions about subjects' performance in a given perceptual modality are not answered in terms of a single summary statistic describing their "real" level of discrimination, but only in terms of a range of detection performances elicited at different criterion positions. That is, in terms of how the subjects' responses to a particular set of stimuli vary over a range of criterion conditions.

In other words, if we were to ask a signal detection theorist, "What is the absolute threshold of hearing for a tone of 2,000 Hz for this person?" we would not receive an apparently precise but actually simplistic answer such as "10 dB". Instead we would receive a graph showing how this person performed under a range of criterion conditions ranging from lax to strict, deriving from a study in which the experimenter had deliberately induced him/her to adopt a range of varying motivational states. If we then looked at these data in dismay, before complaining "Well that's fine; but how can I compare this person's performance with that of someone else?" our S.D. theorist might explain as follows. "Just compare the different graphs. Whilst all the judgements are made in the context of particular criterion states, nonetheless the graphs for different people are not the same shape. Look at these two graphs for example. Whilst I cannot say that either person has a particular threshold, and whilst both subjects' verbal reports vary considerably under different criterion conditions, it is nonetheless the case that this person scores consistently more hits and fewer false positives over the range of conditions than does the other. So I can say with some confidence that his/her hearing (d-prime, in S.D. terminology) is better in that regard."

If we transfer the basic logic of the S.D. experiment into the realm of social research, we should by analogy hesitate about making statements about what a person's "true" or "real" attitude is. Instead we should collect verbal statements from individuals under a range of varying conditions. And when answering questions about which of two individuals has (for example) the most racist attitude we should hesitate to do so in terms of a simple difference between two "true" attitude scores obtained in a single context. Instead we should compare utterances made in a variety of situations, which will reveal that racist statements come more often over a variety of social contexts and conditions from one individual than from the other. Thus we can make useful comparative statements without ever needing to enter into philosophically insoluble debates about whether a particular statement represents or does not represent a "true" attitude or whether a person's "real" attitude is this rather than that. Instead we may postulate differences between individuals in terms of the *variability* of their verbal responses across different *social criterion* conditions.

It is little short of amazing the psychophysicists should have made such progress in coming to terms with the fact that verbal reports a) cannot be taken as perfect representations of internal states, and b) vary as a function of motivational factors extrinsic to the aims and goals of the experiment or study, whilst areas of psychology whose central concern is with verbal reports are still based on assumptions similar to classical psychophysics. The evidence is surely overwhelming that a new paradigm for dealing with verbal reports is overdue, and that any psychology which requires an initial assumption that verbal reports are inherently accurate statements about internal events or entities can no longer be taken as credible. If such a sweeping assertion applies to entire and vast tracts of psychological theory and study, then maybe it is time for a methodological revolution.

5

Social
Criterion Analysis

In the previous chapter we discussed the notion that verbal reports are underlain by a criterion; that is, independent of whatever happens inside the person (indeed, independent of whether *anything* happens) subjects' verbal statements will vary for reasons that concern the consequences of saying one thing rather than another. In the context of an experiment or study, these factors will influence the verbal reports obtained for reasons that may have nothing to do with the subject matter of the study itself. Because of the problems this caused for the classical theory of psychophysics, the theory of signal detection evolved within which these extrinsic motivational or criterion factors were brought into the study in the form of an experimentally manipulated variable. Finally, by way of recapitulation, although psychophysicists have become concerned about criterion effects on verbal reports concerning such uncontentious issues as whether a light is on or not, or a sound is present or not, in areas of social research concerning sensitive and personally involving issues such as drug use, crime, or violence (where a great deal may hang on whether the subject says one thing rather than another) no such theoretical development has taken place. Instead, we have the notion that verbal reports correlate perfectly with, or "perfectly represent", internal events or states (memories, attitudes, beliefs etc.).

It may be suggested therefore that there is a place for the development of a research methodology which attempts to solve criterion problems, first experienced in the perception laboratory, within the more prosaic world of social research in general and drug research in particular. In this chapter an attempt is made to develop a theory of *social criterion* as a factor influencing the nature of socially constituted verbal reports customarily collected in the context of social research. The theory is derived conceptually from the signal-detection theorist's notion of "criterion" but the methodological implications are rather different because of the different natures and purposes of the two research contexts.

What does language mean?

Social research relies heavily on the acceptance of the semantics of verbal reports as representing some form of "truth". This *naive-realistic* view of speech is, not surprisingly therefore, unaccompanied by any particular theory of language since from such a standpoint there is no need for one. It simply means what it says – what a person says they did last week is what they did last week – what a person says they believe is what they believe – and so forth. The quantitative researcher's interpretation of what an utterance means, therefore, is based on the same premises and rules used by the population at large for interpreting verbal statements. Consequently, the statement "I took heroin five times last week" conveys the same information to the layman and to the "expert" alike. What distinguishes the layman from the "scientist" when it comes to social speech acts is not therefore some "deeper" or even "different" understanding of what is said, but some more or less surface methods and techniques for collecting verbal reports economically from large numbers of people, and some statistical methods for turning what they say into numbers which enable comparisons to be made between different groups. This latter is achieved by simplifying speech acts, sometimes to the level of affirmative or negative responses (something that could equally well be achieved by asking subjects to nod or shake their heads), and by suppressing certain sources of individual variability through the use of standardised procedures for collecting and summarising the data. The data obtained from such methods are thus not merely subject to uncontrolled criterion effects, but are also impoverished.

By contrast, those who favour qualitative or ethnographic methods are keenly aware of the artificiality of standard "scientific" methods of data collection, and do in fact seek to explore individual experience within the context of methodologies which require extensive and non standardised conversations with the people involved in the activity in question. Clearly, this solves many of the problems deriving from the artificial (researcher-created) contexts produced by forced-choice or tick-box formats. There is more scope for the elaboration of individual statements about experience and phenomenology and a richer picture emerges. It should be noted however that a richer picture is not necessarily a truer one. The criterion effects referred to above would affect all speech acts of whatever type, however elicited. In other words, the richer and more satisfying individual accounts revealed by qualitative methods are still motivated and selective accounts; and the "expert's" interpretation of the significance of what is said is still basically that of the layman, insofar as no particular theory of socially constituted language *per se* underlies the interpretation.

However, adherents of quantitative and qualitative methods often appear to be driven by the belief that one method or the other will shed light on the "true" nature of attitudes, beliefs, social perceptions, or other states of mind and brain. Advocates of one method or the other are prone to express the belief that their preferred procedure produces not merely a different picture, but a "better" picture of "what is really happening" (see *The Psychologist*, 1992, for an example of such a debate).

Discourse analysts, notable amongst whom are Potter and Wetherell (*op. cit.*), and Edwards and Potter (1992) have pointed out at length the illogicality of such assumptions about the veridical nature of language. Language, they suggest, is always socially constituted, context-bound, and *performative* in the sense that things are said for a purpose; a purpose which is independent of the semantics of what is actually said. That purpose derives from the particular context in which the speech act occurs; and there-fore its precise function is localised and specific to that context. From such a point of view, we must at best leave open to ques-tion the epistemological status of statements about entities such as attitudes, beliefs, recollection or whatever, and seek a method which requires as few assumptions as possible to be made on that front. Unfortunately, while identifying a most fundamental problem, discourse analysts tend to provide virtually nothing that would help towards a principled and replicable method for dealing with discourse (with the possible exception of Potter's Discursive Action Model). Since discourse is bound to context, and its significance is localised to that context, no meta-theory of what an utterance "means" is ever possible. There are simply no extra-linguistic reference points on which to base such a method.

Furthermore, anything analytic or "scientific" that is written about this problem consists in itself of language that is bound by its own localised contextual constraints, in the manner of any other utterance. Therefore, no dispassionate, independent or "expert" interpretations of the problem are possible which might in some sense be taken as fixed markers. All that exists is context-bound discourse whose variability sheds light primarily on the variable nature of discourse, and no light on what people "really mean" (which remains an impossible concept, much like the idea of a "true threshold").

The logic of this argument is compelling; it must surely be "true" at some level at least. However, it is clear that it cannot be either a) the only, or b) the complete picture. It is also clear that if it is "true", then according to its own postulates it cannot be "absolutely" true since it would also be subject to the same type of contextual constraints that affect the material the theory seeks to describe. However it is not necessary at this point to discuss at length whether or not all Greeks are liars, nor what to make of any Greek who tells us that they are, in order to make progress. If my car fails to start and I wish to go to London, I take it to an "expert" and I utter some context bound and performative language such as, "My car won't start". This might or might not be absolutely true, *but I am prepared to accept as fact* the fact or delusion that I am stuck in Kilmarnock with a car that will not go. This perception or delusion is also supported by consensus data of a real or imaginary nature; my wife, or the illusion I take to be my wife, is now producing some context dependent material along the lines "Why haven't you gone yet?" Whether she really exists, or really says that, is more or less irrelevant to the situation I feel myself to be in. Subsequently, the car "expert" tells me some clearly context dependent words which might or might not be true (if he exists) by saying "It's the solenoid. I can fix it in half an hour". The meaning of the statement is localised by a particular set of contextual factors on which I cannot comment. Whether it really is the solenoid or not cannot be known, especially not by me (in truth, the situation is worse than it might be; even if the problem *really* is the solenoid, I am none the wiser. What's a solenoid? It hardly matters whether it is true or not). So without any knowledge of what I am asking, I say "Fix it", whatever that means; and having in fact no idea what "it" is. I imagine that I wait for half an hour; or perhaps I really do; at any rate it feels like half an hour, and my watch (whatever that is) confirms this to my satisfaction at least. And during that time my real or imaginary wife gives me something I take to be a cup of tea. It might of course be a set of spanners (or something that she takes to be set of spanners – she might even be deluded into thinking they are a cup of tea). So long as my wife and I share the same delusion (or my delusional wife shares my delusions) there is no problem. I drink the tea or spanners with one sugar but no milk, and feel better for it or at least think that I do (these two are the same thing aren't they?). Whatever the "truth", eight hours later I am in London talking to the friends I went to see. Or at least, that's what I imagine I am doing. And that, after all, is precisely what I set out to achieve. I can conclude, therefore, that regardless of whether any of it is "true" or not, it works for me. Consequently, whether or not the world actually exists, far from being a crucial problem, is a supreme irrelevance. I suppose it would be nice to think that I really did go to London and talk to some real friends, but it doesn't actually make that much difference.

However, the discourse analyst's position is perhaps not that the world does not exist, but that it exists only as a linguistically mediated social construction. From such a standpoint, there is no absolute "truth", but only relative meanings that are localised by context. Once again, this must be right. But far from being a fundamental obstacle, it is another irrelevance. Provided that either existentially or in fact, by exchanging some verbal material of unknown epistemological status, my car starts and I go, in my mind at least, to London there is no difficulty. We have exchanged some words whose truthfulness is unknowable, but whose utility is beyond dispute. The car seemed to start and appeared to take me to London. All that is necessary, therefore, is that speech be utilitarian; that it helps in solving problems. Difficulties only arise when particular groups of people assume or insist that their way of going about such problem-solving exercises is the only "true" one. Perhaps the problem arises indirectly from the argument that because the meaning of language is always contextually defined, we cannot make simplistic use of language to shed light on the "true" nature of entities-in-the-head such as beliefs, attitudes, norms, or any of the other members of that army of non-parsimonious constructs invented by psychologists. This seems a very compelling argument. It does not follow from this, however, that because language can shed no light on such internal processes or states, that no processes or states exist. It merely means that it is going to be hard to find out what they are simply by asking questions and assuming the answers have perfect face validity.

It is pertinent to ask the question at this point, "What does it matter whether what I or anyone else says is absolute truth, or merely context dependent performative construction, so long as certain individual or shared goals are achieved?" My general aim in life is not to go around telling people the way the world really is, which would restrict me to primarily evangelical utterings such as "The End of the World is Nigh", or "Man is Conceived in Sin", but to say things that will be of utilitarian value with respect to certain goals I wish to achieve. Presumably the major purpose of language is to facilitate exactly such processes, rather than merely to serve as a sort of verbal information highway or fact sheet. Within that context, a statement such as "I am addicted to heroin" would not be seen primarily as a statement of some "truth" about the way the world is. It might or might not be. But it is certainly a motivated and context dependent utterance which has the performative aim of achieving certain goals. Without disagreeing with the basics of Potter and Wetherell's ideas about the nature of language, we can therefore say that if language is performative then we may at least try to relate what is said to the aims it seeks to achieve. In other words we are entitled to research one entity in the mind/brain; namely purposiveness or if you prefer, motivation. If people say things for reasons shaped by a particular context, we may hypothesise about what the reasons are and then see whether in fact that context produces the predicted functional type of discourse. If we are successful, furthermore, we do not have to claim that the papers and theoretical articles emerging from the theory show that the theory is real or "true"; we merely need to insist that the theory is useful and that it helps us solve salient problems. And similarly, an "expert" is not someone who knows a "truth" that is unknown to the rest of us, (indeed, such a notion places the "expert" in the role of prophet or soothsayer) but rather someone who comes up with context bound and performative utterances that help us solve problems more frequently that do the utterances of other "non-experts".

Whilst Potter is unhappy about the postulation of *any* entities in the brain (personal communication – phone call) the current theory of social criterion requires that we assume different motivational states really exist within different people, and it is these differing motivations expressed within a variety of contexts in varying ways that actually give rise to the problems Potter *et al.* seek to address in the first place. If people were not motivated to achieve certain aims and goals, it is hard to see how one could have a performative or functional theory of language at all. In fact, Potter *et al.* denial of any entities-in-the-brain, up to and including motivation, cannot be sustained. Their own work, on which their radical and challenging conclusions are based, is redolent with reference to factors which can only be termed "motivational". Consider the following extract, appearing under the heading `Function, construction and variation' (1987, *op. cit.*, pp. 32-33).

> "*One of the themes strongly stressed by both speech act theory and ethnomethodology was that people use their language to DO things: to order and request, persuade and accuse. This focus on language function is also one of the major components of discourse analysis. Function, however, cannot be understood in a mechanical way. Unfortunately, as we all know, when people are persuading, accusing, requesting etc. they do not always do so explicitly. When someone makes a request – perhaps they want to borrow your calculator – they do not always politely but explicitly ask; `could I borrow your calculator this evening, please?' Often they are less direct than this, perhaps couching the request as an abstract question: `would you mind if I borrowed your calculator this evening?' or even more obliquely: `it is going to drive me mad doing all those statistics by hand tonight' (Brown & Levinson, 1978). It may be to the speaker's advantage to make a request indirectly because it allows the recipient to reject it without making the rejection obvious (Drew, 1984). On the whole, people prefer to head off undesirable acts like rejections before they happen (Drew, 1986; and see chapter Four)*" [all references are cited in the source text]

It is difficult to see how one could maintain a non-motivational standpoint whilst still writing in the above manner. In the above extract, not only is there a clear motive on one side to borrow a calculator (an explicit motive which determines the denotative and operational content of the utterance), but there is a hierarchy of motives. The speaker is also motivated to avoid a direct refusal (a non-explicit motive which primarily influences the manner of expression). Interestingly and importantly, the first motive (to borrow the calculator) is explicit in the surface meaning of the language use; whilst the second motive (to avoid a direct refusal) is NOT so reflected. Instead, this second-order motive clearly determines the way the first-order motive is expressed, but in itself this second motive is unstated. In other words, whilst one motive emerges clearly in terms of a consensual understanding of "what the words mean", the second does not. Potter thus not only discusses two levels of motivation for the utterance; he is able to provide a hypothesis about non-stated motives from the manner in which the question is posed, as opposed to its literal semantic content. This is a crucial point we shall elaborate later. Finally, the last sentence in the above quotation (*"On the whole, people prefer to head off undesirable acts...*) is clearly a reference to motivational states, and it could only be an act of obstinacy to write such a sentence whilst simultaneously insisting that the notion of motive cannot be employed.

Before describing social criterion analysis in specific detail, it is worth looking at one more quote from Potter *et al.,* since at this point his conclusions appear to be very much in line with the current argument. They write (*op. cit.,* pp. 33):

> *"In general, we find that if talk is oriented to many different functions, global and specific, any examination of language over time reveals considerable VARIATION. A person's account will vary according to its function. That is, it will vary according to the purpose of the talk."*

In the next section, we will discuss the type of variability described above by Potter *et al.* and will attempt by means of social criterion analysis to come to terms with that variability. Subsequently, in the next chapter, we shall apply the second assertion of Potter *et al.,* that accounts vary according to function over time, to the development of a discursive theory of "drugspeak" to show such changes over time; and also to show that such changes are orderly, recognisable, and analysable in terms of motive, in exactly the way that Potter attributes second-order motives to his would-be calculator borrower.

The first step, then, is to see whether any progress can be made with the notion of "social criterion", and whether we can envisage a set of methods for dealing with verbal data that take into account different motivational states and contextual effects, after the manner of signal detection theory. The answer to this problem is, in the opinion of this author, an affirmative one, and an account of the detailed methodology proposed is given in Davies and Best (1995) on which the following paragraphs are closely based. The method makes a loose analogy with certain of the concepts underlying signal detection theory, including subject criterion as described above; but it also takes on board the idea of science as a highly interested rhetorical practice (rather than the objective and disinterested pursuit of truth) by using the notion of signal-strength as an indicant of the *researcher's motivation to find out certain things rather than others*. At the end of the day, data are evaluated in terms of their "robustness", which is the extent to which the same, or a different, picture emerges as a consequence of changes in the researcher's chosen method and alterations to the context of the study. The assumption is that verbal reports will be sensitive to differences in methodology and context, insofar as such differences prompt changes in the functionality of certain types of response; rather than the assumption that verbal report data represent fixed or categorical data retrieved from storage in an unmotivated fashion in response to questions which appear (are assumed to appear) disinterested (e.g. "remember, there are no right or wrong answers..."), objective ("... this test is known to have high validity and reliability") and neutral ("I am just a research scientist... so I have no opinions either way on what you say").

Let us now recap some of the main points made so far. In research into the problems of addiction, but also in many other areas of research concerning health and social issues, verbal reports are used in an attempt to access and describe states of affairs as if they were, literally, stored data inside people's heads. Asking a question, giving out a questionnaire, requesting short answers "in your own words", are all seen as methods which are analogous to pressing the necessary buttons on a computer in order to retrieve data from storage; only in this instance "data" are assumed to have been "retrieved" from "storage" inside a person instead of from a machine. It is argued that this analogy is false, and that verbal behaviour like other behaviours is motivated and serves purposes for the individual.* Furthermore, it is context dependent,

---

*Within the scientific process, that data one collects to support a theory depend on how one conceptualises the problem in the first place; consequently they can only support or refute that conceptualisation. It is observed that when people are asked to produce verbal reports about mental processes, they do so. This is generally conceptualised as a deep-freeze process; things are stored inside people's heads, and they retrieve them when required to do so. It can also be conceptualised as an electrical generator analogy. Electricity comes out of a generator, but there is no electricity inside it. It is eminently reasonable to commence from the standpoint that brains are primarily generative, rather than store-houses. From such a standpoint, any edifice built around retrieval in any literal sense looks problematic.

with people saying different things for different reasons in differing circumstances. Even though particular methods or scales may have "proven reliability" this merely attests to the fact that the scales produce the same results, when administered in the same way in the same context, and not to their "truth". An alternative, if somewhat anarchistic, way of viewing reliability is as a measure of a test's capacity to reproduce at time `b' the same artefacts and context specific utterances it produced at time `a'. (If this is overstating the argument, one could certainly qualify it by saying that IF a test produces nonsense at time `a', then high reliability is a definite disadvantage. At least an unreliable test might work sometimes.)

Validity is taken to be the indicant of "truth", but this frequently means that the particular test in question produces results similar to verbal reports obtained in similar contexts elsewhere, using similar tests; though, admittedly, validity estimates in some areas are often based on non-verbally mediated behavioural outcomes. However, when dealing with "mental entities" whose existence is inferred solely on the basis of verbal reports, the external validity of such "measures" is impossible to ascertain since private and unobservable entities or processes are involved, with the verbal data constituting the primary (or only) evidence of their "existence".

This is not to suggest, however, that verbal reports are therefore irrelevant, but simply that it is unnecessary to make assumptions about the extent to which they represent, or do not represent, some stable mentalistic substrate in order to make progress. Verbal reports sometimes predict behaviour, and very frequently they do not. These are (appear to be) empirical facts, and whether or not the verbal reports of attitudes, intentions or whatever reflect the status of some internal "state of affairs" is largely irrelevant to the findings of links between what people say and what they do.

Socially constituted verbal reports, viewed as psychophysics

In a previous section, the point was made that researchers tend to assume a correlation of 1 between verbal reports and some presumed objective reality or state of affairs. This assumption, we noted, resembles one of the main assumptions of classical psychophysics, namely that reports of internal events and the internal events themselves correlate perfectly. We have seen how this assumption was proved to be untenable within the context of psychophysical experiments (the data clearly showed variability in subject reporting; they did not give the same verbal response to the same stimulus over an entire trial series) and how the theory of signal detection evolved as way of dealing with this difficulty. Psychophysicists produced the notion of "criterion" (known in S.D. parlance as "beta") a subject variable quite distinct from "d-prime" which is a measure of the detectability of the stimulus. In other words, whether subjects reported detecting the stimulus or not depended on rather more than the strength of the stimulus; it was also a function of the subjects' criterion.

In an S.D. experiment, the subjects' criterion for reporting the presence or absence of a stimulus is varied by the simple expedient of attaching costs and benefits to the different possible response alternatives; in the case of a simple threshold study, these alternatives would basically be "yes" or "no". This, at risk of stating the obvious, affects the subject's motivational state, and hence the relative probabilities of their answering "Yes I see it" as opposed to "No I don't". For example, if a subject is rewarded with money every time he/she scores a HIT (i.e. correctly says "yes" when a stimulus is presented) a lax criterion is produced whereby the subject becomes more likely to say "yes" whatever the circumstances. Under a lax criterion, therefore, the subject will detect stimuli not previously detected, and under extreme circumstances will even detect signals that were not actually presented. Note that the question, "Yes, but did he/she REALLY detect it?" is simply not answerable, and has no place in this paradigm. The data are hard, and consist entirely of observable response probabilities derived under a range of conditions, requiring no acts of faith by way of assumptions about the relationship of verbal reports to "what really happened inside".

By contrast, if money is taken off subjects for FALSE POSITIVES, a stricter criterion position is adopted. A false positive occurs whenever the subject says "yes" to a signal that was not presented. Initially it may strike the reader as incredible that a person would report seeing or hearing something that was not in fact there except on the rarest occasions, but this is not the case. In fact, people commonly produce false positives in all sorts of situations. Imagine what an S.D. experiment would be like. First, there will be many repeated trials. If a signal is presented on all or most of the trials, this in itself leads the subject to EXPECT a signal to occur, thus increasing the likelihood of a "yes" response. On the other hand, if there are a great many no-signal trials, the subject becomes more likely to MISS a signal when it is presented. Furthermore, if the signals themselves are of low detectability, this increases the subject's uncertainty about saying "yes" or "no" since the difference between signal-present and signal-absent is harder to discriminate. Consequently, given a series of hard-to-detect stimuli in a study which has many signal-present trials, FALSE POSITIVES will be common under a lax criterion.

However, as noted at the top of the above paragraph, a strict criterion can be induced by punishing false positive responses, perhaps by taking money off people. Under such circumstances, subjects produce fewer "yes" responses overall, and will therefore be more inclined to miss signals that they may have previously detected under a more lax criterion. Indeed, if the penalties are sufficiently fierce, subjects will only have the confidence to say "yes" to the most blatant signals.

We can summarise the philosophy of S.D. theory by quoting a couple of extracts from McNicol's (1972) primer of signal detection. He writes (page 10):

> *"another interesting feature of signal detection theory, from a psychological point of view, is that it is concerned with decisions based on evidence which does not unequivocally support one out of a number of hypotheses. More often than not, real-life decisions have to be made on the weight of the evidence and with some uncertainty, rather than on evidence which clearly supports one line of action to the exclusion of all others."*

And later (p. 11):

> *"Essentially, the measures allow us to separate two aspects of an observer's decision. The first of these is called* **sensitivity,** *that is how well the observer is able to make correct judgements and avoid incorrect ones. The second of these is called* **bias,** *that is, the extent to which the observer favours one hypothesis over another independent of the evidence he has been given."*

Whilst McNicol is referring to sensory evidence about the presentation of signals in a laboratory experiment, and whilst he rides rough-shod over some of the philosophical problems raised earlier (the assumption that "correct judgement" about internal states represents some sort of achievable gold-standard), the underlying principles clearly have implications beyond the walls of the perception laboratory. Note the reference to "real-life decisions" and the observer who "favours one hypothesis over another".

The fit between the philosophy of S.D. and certain "real life" situations is rather startling. Consider the social worker under pressure not to MISS any cases of child abuse (that is, motivated to score more HITS) confronted with highly ambiguous information; a situation in which, due to a reduction in criterion strictness, more correct identifications (HITS) will be made at the cost of more incorrect or inappropriate identifications (FALSE POSITIVES). Or perhaps the psychologist, seeking evidence to support a favourite theory of stress, who unwittingly adopts a research method which induces a lax criterion for the self-reporting of stress, or sends a very clear "signal" that self-reports of stress are required (i.e. a questionnaire with "Stress Survey" written in big letters on the front). The implications are disquieting.

Social Criterion (S.C.) Theory

We assume at the outset that the subjects in a social psychology experiment or study possess social motives that influence the probability of obtaining different verbal responses from them; and that this is analogous to the S.D. notion of "criterion". We also assume, in accordance with a reflexive philosophy, that the researcher has motives which influence the outcome of a study. Thus, if, as Higgins and Bargh (1987) suggest, even subtle priming manipulations can influence such things as the reporting of attitudes, any study henceforth has to include a measure of the researcher's motivation before the results can be interpreted. Within the proposed "social criterion theory", such "priming manipulations" are seen as a loose analogy to the strength of the signals which the experimenter decides to use in an S.D. study; other things being equal (e.g. criterion) sending stronger signals produces more HITS. By making this distinction it becomes possible we believe, to separate out subject criterion from the surface meaning of what is said.

However, there are problems with the analogy at this point. If we wish to pursue the S.D. analogy between searching for a light or a sound amongst background noise, and "searching for" a memory (attitude, opinion, or whatever we wish to call it) in a sea of cognitive background noise, or if we merely wish to view verbal reports as context-cued or functional discursive acts, the analogy itself has to suggest practical new ways of proceeding or else it merely remains an idle curiosity. In an S.D. study, as we noted above, criterion is manipulated by attaching rewards and punishments to HITS and FALSE POSITIVES. Adapting this to verbal reports in the context of a piece of social research suggests rather a bizarre procedure. We should, by analogy, encourage the subject to remember or report (detect) certain things on some trials by providing rewards, and on other trials we should punish "false positives"; and in this way develop a separation of criterion (motivation) from detectability. Furthermore, the S.D. model suggests the need for large numbers of repeated trials. In a social context, this appears to require us to measure someone's "attitude" over and over again, possibly hundreds of times, under different reinforcement conditions, a requirement that destroys utterly any sense of social reality or ecological validity that the study might otherwise have possessed.

Despite these problems, however, the analogy is useful. For example, giving evidence in a court of law, as opposed to recounting the same incident to friends at home, might be expected to produce accounts which differ in emphasis and mode of expression, since the rewards and punishments for particular pieces of discourse differ between the two situations. Thus, we might observe that a drug user attributes an illegal act to "addiction" when in the courtroom, but gives an account characterised by volition and bad luck when talking to his/her friends. If this were observed to be a general phenomenon, one might infer a context-based motivational shift on the part of the drug using defendant; in the courtroom the criterion for reporting "addiction" is lax and consequently the number of FALSE POSITIVES (reporting "addiction" where there is no "addiction") will he high in that setting. Further if one accepts the notion of Eiser *et al.,* (1985) that the "addiction" explanation can be socially generated and has significant consequences for those who self-attribute in this way, its *pattern of variability between contexts,* by providing clues to motivation, may have predictive value for future behaviour that exceeds that of any individual act of "measurement". Despite the difficulties of operationalising certain S.D. concepts, the notion of "criterion" thus seems to make intuitive sense at least within the social research context.

What about signal strength, and detectability? Consider a "life events" study in which subjects have to provide a researcher with information about negative events that occurred during some time period prior to the interview. It is observed that more such events are reported by subjects when using a forced-choice check-list on which subjects tick off any events that have happened to them, than when they are asked the open-ended question "Tell me anything important that happened to you in the last month". In unpublished research by Shibli (1992) the open-ended question elicited a mean of 7 events from drug users, whilst a check-list of some 100 events produced a mean of 49. In such circumstances, the question "Which is the true answer" is misconceived, in exactly the same way as the classical notion of "threshold" is misconceived. No single data set can be treated in isolation from the circumstances under which it was elicited; a postulate which, however unlikely it may seem, lies at the heart of both discourse analysis and signal detection theory. In terms of our proposed social criterion theory, the two methods are deemed to differ in *signal strength,* a variable that is set by the researcher. Consequently, the method used becomes the measure of the researcher's own motivation. Thus, if the researcher requires evidence of many negative life events, the check-list is the approach to use since *this sends the strongest signal.* The check-list specifically and comprehensively defines the "signals" which the subject must search for while the free recall method gives no such clues, so there is less certainty. Naturally, it goes without saying that people will generally find the things you want if you tell them what to look for; whether the objects are hard-boiled eggs, memories of hard-boiled eggs or supposed attitudes to hard-boiled eggs. The notion of signal strength thus becomes crucial in social criterion theory, since the methodology used could in principal give a measure of the researcher's own motivation in carrying out the study.

One can say therefore, that within social criterion theory, as in signal detection, higher rates of HITS *must* be accompanied by more FALSE POSITIVES, other things being equal. Thus, if the psychologist deliberately sets out to design an interviewing situation that is more conducive to certain types of self disclosure, this motivated manipulation by the psychologist will affect all subjects and increase the rate of such self-disclosure overall. Most psychologists would probably accept that such a manipulation was a motivated act on their part; but fewer would perhaps accept that this manipulation of context could have an impact on all those interviewed and not just those with "something to tell"; and perhaps fewer still would be happy with the idea that, given a highly conducive situation and a relatively rare phenomenon, the "conducive" situation could yield less overall "truth" than a "non-conducive" situation (i.e. there is a point at which false positives exceed the real base rate in the population, at which point more harm than good is done). Furthermore, the choice of a measurement method that sends strong signals (e.g. a forced-choice check-list questionnaire with the title of the subject matter printed in large letters on the front) will elicit more reports of the phenomenon in question than a method that sends fewer cues and has a less-identifiably specific theme. Given these variables, the best summary of the verbal reports of any individual will not arise from any specific one of these situations or methods, but from the variability of the subject's responses over all of them in the manner of an ROC curve.

So how does one apply the specifics of S.D. theory to social research, given the intuitive sense it makes of many situations?

Criterion for response (beta)

Within the context of an S.D. experiment, this is generally manipulated by a) attaching rewards to HITS and/or punishments to FALSE POSITIVES, and b) varying the probability of occurrence of the signal, thereby manipulating subjects' expectations, as described previously.

Within the proposed Social Criterion (S.C.) theory, many repeated trials of the type necessitated by S.D. studies threaten to destroy the ecological validity (social reality) of any data collection exercise. We have to make do, therefore, with many fewer trials; two repetitions are suggested here. On the basis of two repetitions, exact estimates of criterion cannot be made, but we can at least observe the *direction of any shift,* and whether similar shifts are made by significant proportions of any subject group. If this is acceptable, then the aim becomes to change subject motivation between interviews, and thereby alter the criterion for response. This might be done by employing different interviewers with contrasting styles and affiliations (see Davies & Baker, 1987), by providing different information, different schedules, different physical environments, in short by varying the two data collection exercises in any of a number of ways, *according to a clear theory-led hypothesis*. The aim at the outset would be to have two different rounds of data collection, and to provide differing degrees or types of contextual cueing. The experimenter is required to have a hypothesis about the two contexts such that he/she can predict the direction of criterion shift as revealed in the verbal reports. If the verbal reports shift in the *direction* predicted, the experimenter has data which are consistent with the hypothesis, and thus on the type of reports a given context is likely to elicit; in other words the experimenter understands how the contexts involved affect people. On the other hand, if the shift in verbal report does not accord with the prediction, the experimenter does not understand the context shift, nor its impact upon people. The approach contrasts with more traditional approaches (e.g. Katz, 1960) in that no intra-psychic mediation between context and account is posited or required. Instead, this issue remains open; all that is assumed is that certain contexts produce certain types of verbal report for whatever reason. The model is thus compatible with a variety of different assumptions about the link between verbal report and behaviour.

Let us take a concrete example. Suppose that in the context of an interview with drug users *carried out by* a known drug user in a public house, drug users gave accounts of themselves characterised by fewer drug-related problems, less intense patterns of use, greater control and more positive affect (more fun), than in the context of an interview conducted by a suit-wearing psychologist in a formal institutional setting (see for example Davies & Baker, *op. cit.*). Applying the proposed S.C. model to this study requires a hypothesis that, in the latter of the two contexts, a more lax criterion will be adopted with respect to the reporting of "addiction" problems. This hypothesis might derive from evidence supporting the idea that drug users' motivation is more defensive in formal settings involving establishment figures than in less formal settings involving members of their own peer group. This hypothesis can be tested by looking at how answers in fact change between the two settings. If the data support the hypothesis, an understanding develops about the impact of certain contextual frames on drug users without any reference to "truth" or "reality", or underlying attitudes as revealed in any particular piece of discourse.

Signal strength

There is no way of manipulating signal strength in a manner that would satisfy a hard-line signal-detection theorist. However, the interviewer has the option of bringing certain issues into salience (for example, by the use of forced-choice check-lists, or agree/disagree questions, or other forms which explicitly describe the "signal" to be searched for); or of not bringing them into salience (as in open-ended methods). To the extent that subjects are more certain that a particular type of signal is the one to be searched for, its strength relative to other signals may be said to be enhanced. Within S.D. theory, the notion of "salience" would probably be seen as a criterion issue, but within the context of the proposed model, criterion issues involve subject motivation (see above) whereas signal strength is here conceptualised as a function of the *researcher's* motivation. In sum, signal strength here represents the degree of salience attached to a particular issue by the person carrying out the study.

Defined in such a way, signal strength refers to the emphasis given to a particular issue within the data collection methodology. Highly explicit questionnaires with forced-choice alternatives provide a strong signal as to what is required; semi-structured or open-ended procedures provide a less-strong signal. From this point of view, data collected by different methods can be used to assess the impact of high v. low levels of signal on the nature of the verbal reports obtained. Where contrasting methods produce basically the same data, one must conclude that the internal signal is strong for the subject i.e. his/her motivation (criterion) remains constant across methods independent of the experimenter's attempts to influence it. Thus someone suffering a recent bereavement will probably recall that event regardless of the method used, indicating high salience for the subject. On the other hand, events that are only recalled in response to explicit prompts or closed formats may be assumed to be of lower subjective salience, assuming no other shifts to the context of responding.

For example, a check-list survey of life stress, in which people tick off stressful events from a list provided by the experimenter should be interpreted in the light of a second round of data collection collected by less structured means. If the stressors reported are salient for the person in question, the difference between the data produced by the two methods will be minimised; whereas substantial differences in the data produced by the different methods reveal that there is a difference in the strength of the signal that the two data collection methods constitute. In this latter case, we would not conclude that the subject's motivation (or attitude, or whatever) had changed, but merely that the data were not robust across methods.

Order effects

From the above discussions of criterion and signal strength, it can be seen that, in statistical terms, reliable criterion shifts would be revealed by significant main effects for context, whilst shifts in signal strength would be revealed by significant main effects for method. A variety of standard experimental designs is thus suggested by this conceptual framework. There is however one caveat deriving from empirical work which places limits on the types of design that should be employed. It is tempting to forge ahead with designs involving two contexts, and two contrasting methods, arranged within a design that controls for order-effects. For example, half the subjects might receive open-ended followed by forced-choice formats; with the remaining subjects receiving forced-choice followed by open-ended. Such a design might be calculated to eliminate order effects, but such an assumption would, it appears, be wrong. The order effect is not reflexive; that is, the effect of a) on b) is not equal and opposite to the effect of b) on a). In a recent evaluation of a drug project (Fast Forward) situated in Leith, an attempt was made to utilise some of the concepts of social criterion theory. Data were collected in different contexts, and in addition a forced-choice diagnostic questionnaire was paired with an open-ended discussion of personal problems and drug related activities (Best, Mortimer, MacMillan & Davies, 1995). Half the subjects received the questionnaire first and open-ended interview second; and half received these in the opposite order. Subsequent analysis revealed a measurable and sometimes striking impact of the forced-choice questionnaire upon subsequent open-ended discussions. This is an important finding, since at present there is a vogue amongst researchers to make use of both qualitative and quantitative methods; and for some reason, many researchers prefer to collect the structured data first, and the qualitative data second. The findings from the

Fast Forward project clearly indicate the reflexive nature of social research. Filling in a structured questionnaire is not simply a data collecting exercise; it is also a teaching exercise. The subjects in the study learn about the beliefs, assumptions and broader agenda of the researcher from the type of questions they are asked to respond to. In the present instance, after having completed a questionnaire dealing with a variety of drug problems/symptoms, most of the positive reference to drug use was eliminated from subsequent discussions, which tended to focus on the "bad" aspects of drug use. If this finding is valid, the specific implication is that unstructured methods should always precede structured. The broader implication is that repeated filling in of diagnostic or screening questionnaires may have hitherto unforeseen implications for the filler-in, and the way he/she comes to view their drug use, and how they describe it to others.

Signal to noise ratio

It is possible to go beyond signal strength and make some comments about s/n ratio, although the applicability of the S.D. analogy becomes more problematic at this point. By varying the *content* of the protocols we use, we can attempt to increase or decrease the salience of competing cognitions, or the likelihood of obtaining particular species of discourse (choose whichever conceptualisation you prefer), by looking at the effects of such manipulations on the verbal reports obtained. If the analogy is accepted, s/n ratio can be specified as the ratio of target-to-non-target questions contained in the protocol. A target question would be one which was identifiable in terms of its surface semantics as belonging to that subset of questions concerned with the topic of the research. A non-target question would not be so identifiable.

For example, a research project into teenage drinking might involve questions directly concerned with that topic (When did you last have a drink? How often do you drink? What did you drink last Tuesday? etc.) and other questions not related to drinking; that is, so-called filler questions, traditionally supposed to take the subject's mind off the real purpose of the exercise and thus avoid defensive reactions (though the logic of this has never been clear to this author, as it seems to assume some sort of subliminal perception effect). One could thus in principle vary the proportions, and express these as the s/n ratio. Consequently, at one extreme would be the questionnaire made up entirely of drink-related questions, and at the other would be the absurd drinking questionnaire, which asked no drink-related questions at all. S/n ratio is thus, in principle, easily specified.

There are problems, however. Certain versions of the questionnaire become increasingly cost-ineffective as more and more data are collected on topics that are irrelevant; whilst on the other hand, "tokenism" is a real problem also. Tokenism in this context consists of sticking in a number of assorted questions on the assumption that a few verbal feints and bodyswerves will be sufficient to confuse the subject as to the real purpose of the exercise. Unfortunately they are not so easily fooled, according to two studies which have examined this effect. Two studies have examined this "tokenism" problem. The first, by Davies and Stacey (1972), included a section on "hobbies and pastimes" in a survey of teenage drinking. Studies of the ad lib comments made by the teenagers in a last open-ended section showed that few were beguiled into thinking the study was about anything other than drinking. In a broadly similar study by Plant and Miller (1977) a survey was presented as either a study of drinking or of leisure pursuits. The data again revealed that this type of manipulation can be discouragingly transparent.

Notwithstanding the practical problems of s/n ratio, we can still speculate that the detectability of certain signals will be greater where noise is lower, and less where noise is greater. And as in the case of signal strength, data which remain constant when s/n ratio is drastically changed from high (e.g. a set consisting of all-target questions except one) to low (a set of non-target questions containing one target question) may be assumed to be salient or "highly detectable" for the individual concerned. We might even go so far as to speculate that the statement "I sometimes experience problems with my drinking" will have less predictive value for future behaviour if it only emerges from a check-list of alcohol problems than if it is selected from a broad ranging set of topics of which alcohol is only one. In such a case, since the s/n ratio is low (i.e. there is a lot of noise) we would also anticipate fewer positive responses. The idea of exchanging a larger number of positive responses with relatively poor prediction, for fewer positives and better prediction, is open to empirical examination and cost benefit analysis.

Implications of the model: methodological

The model requires a more sophisticated approach to the design of data collection exercises than is usually the case with traditional methods.

Firstly, assessment of criterion (beta) requires two episodes of data collection in contrasting contexts, which can theoretically be expected to alter subject motivation in predictable ways (prediction in this sense meaning *a priori* prediction on the basic of a hypothesis; not the kind of *ex post facto* prediction which can be trawled from any data set by the atheoretical mass-application of regression-based statistics). This contradicts a certain received wisdom that requires all data to be collected in a standard way in order to remove bias. In fact, such a procedure does not remove bias, but rather ensures that whatever bias is present will go undetected.

The nature of the contexts to be studied depends on the theory from which prediction is being derived. It might involve different interviewers or different physical situations but it might involve something as simple as revealing at a second interview how the interviewer rated the subject at a first interview (see for example, McAllister and Davies 1992). Similarly, in the *Scottish National Evaluation of Drug Education*, Coggans *et al.*, (1991), collected data in two contrasting ways (i.e. suit-wearing data collectors using a formal questionnaire *versus* fringed-jacket/jeans/Doc Martens-wearing data collectors using a questionnaire with street language and cartoons). Data that remained unchanged under this manipulation were assumed to be robust; data that changed were seen to be context-dependent. Data which were found to be robust across contexts were assumed to be a more useful description of the study, and similar groups, than data that were context-specific.

Secondly, given that two contexts have been specified, and that a prediction of their impact upon subjects' discourse has been made in the light of some theory, then assessment of signal strength requires two methods of data elicitation to be employed in each context. As mentioned previously, it is important to proceed from a less structured to a more structured approach rather than the other way around; our data suggesting that structured approaches bring the researcher's agenda into salience, a persisting effect which contaminates subsequent less-structured (open-ended; qualitative or whatever) methods of data collection.

Since, as indicated above, the distinction between signal strength and s/n ratio can become somewhat arbitrary in terms of specifying the discursive context within which a central item appears, the separate issue of s/n ratio will be excluded for the present. Work is in progress on clarifying these issues, as well as into ways of producing an ROC curve for social discourses. The question of a possible interaction between signal strength and s/n ratio is in principle amenable to empirical study, but further speculation at this point in unlikely to enhance the clarity of the analogy. For the moment it is sufficient to suggest that manipulating signal strength or s/n ratio in the ways suggested can be collectively viewed as ways of attempting to assess salience or "detectability".

Implications of the model: data/theoretical

At the present time, qualitative and quantitative methods have tended to polarise, and each has its earnest devotees. However, within the proposed theory of social criterion, they both become subsumed under the same model. Within that model, they simply promote different criterion positions and offer different signal strengths, with neither having any particular claim to "truth" or "reality" that the other does not. Anyone wishing to do so could thus set up the two methodologies as reference points, and use the differences in the data they produce as the outcome variable in some hypothesis testing exercise. In such an exercise, reports could be assumed to have reality or "truth" for the contexts in which they occurred, and under the methods used to elicit them, without any damage to the underlying model. This does not require some form of radical relativism, nor total social constructionism, but merely recognises and takes on board the blatantly obvious fact that people say different things in different situations, for reasons the experimenter may not know anything about. Any method which requires a denial of this fact, and suggests instead that one particular method in one context is the fount of a particular psychological "truth" is surely no longer acceptable. Instead, an overall framework is required that takes into account the contextuality of verbal reports and the localised epistemology that must be the foundation for the interpretation of the motives that underly them.

Implications of the model: practical

Since application of this model requires a minimum of two contexts for data collection, and at least two research methods with differing signal strengths, research based on the collection and analysis of verbal reports becomes at least four times more costly for any given sample size. It must be remembered however that the basic postulates for mental measurement derive from the early years of this century, and notions of physical science that even physicists no longer accept (see chapter 1). Whilst major conceptual and technological advances have been made in other areas of science, the classic Thurstone-type conceptualisation of attitudes as something existing inside people's head over time, amenable to direct and concrete one-off measurement of the type one might use to measure the size of a table top, has remained basically unaltered for sixty years. Admittedly, new methods cost more money; but the alternative idea that research which actually informs public policy can be satisfactorily conducted on a shoestring budget, and involve nothing more than asking people some one-off and highly directive questions in a theoretical vacuum, is not acceptable. Small wonder that, despite all our endeavours, the problems of drug misuse continue to escalate; the natural history and functions of drug discourse have never even been described. So it's going to cost a little bit more, and take longer to do. But can we afford to base public policy with respect to key issues on outdated concepts and methods? And it goes without saying that the cost of a single particle accelerator would probably fund all the research into everyday problems of existence for the next decade.

An Example

It is proposed at this stage to provide an interpretation of a study by McAllister and Davies (*op. cit.*), as an illustration of how a study might be designed that fits in with the postulates of social criterion theory. The aim is to provide an impression of how such a study might be designed, how results might be interpreted, and how little is actually sacrificed by suspension of the belief that such studies have to pursue "truth" in order to answer important questions.

Theoretical basis

Conceptions about the nature of drug addiction draw in large part from the verbal reports of problem drug users. The reports characterise addiction as being a state in which control of behaviour and volition are lost, and where behaviour becomes basically "drug driven". However, attribution theory (See the *Myth of Addiction op. cit.*) provides a body of evidence suggesting that explanations of drug use might be primarily functional rather than veridical. This body of theory suggests that reports of addicted behaviour from drug users may follow certain functional predictions of attribution theory rather than being "true statements". The body of research in attribution theory thus provides the theoretical basis for a hypothesis.

Hypothesis

On the basis of certain findings from the area of attribution theory it is predicted that drug users who receive information that a psychologist *has a particular view of them* will make attributional statements which are functional in terms of that (i.e. the psychologist's) view. Specifically, in the context of a repeated measures design, it is predicted that an "addicted" style of explanation will be consequent upon the classification of a person's drug use as "heavy", whereas a "non-addicted" style of explanation will accompany the classification of their drug use as "light".

Criterion

A study is devised in which feedback is given to smokers about how the psychologist has categorised their smoking behaviour; and two contexts are devised to detect possible changes in their verbal reports. A group of smokers is interviewed at Time 1, and their attributions for smoking are noted. Data on their self-reported consumption are also taken by asking them to complete a one-week retrospective smoking diary, although no assumptions are necessary about the "truthfulness" or otherwise of these consumption reports within this paradigm. The group is subsequently dichotomised at the median in terms of their reported consumption, to form a heavy-smoking and a light-smoking group. At Time 2, the interview is repeated, but on this occasion, the heavy-smokers are informed that they have been assigned to this category, and the words "heavy smoker" appear at the top of each page of the protocol. The light smokers are informed that they have been assigned to a light-smoking category and the words "light smoker" appear at the top of each page of the protocol. Attributions for smoking are then collected again. *In one subset of data* (this issue is clarified in the next paragraph) it is observed that smokers classified as "heavy smokers" show attributional shifts towards a more "addicted" style of explanation (internal, stable, uncontrollable) at the second interview, whilst those classified as "light smokers" shift towards a "non-addicted" style of explanation. There is a statistically significant difference between the heavy and light smoking groups at Time 2, but not at Time 1.

Signal strength

At each interview, two data collection procedures are adopted. One involves the unstructured elicitation of natural attributions for smoking, minimally cued by a number of open-ended "why" type questions. The other involves the use of a standard forced-choice questionnaire and rating scales for measuring drug-use attributions developed by McAllister from previous work by Weiner. It is observed that the criterion shift described in the previous paragraph is specific to the questionnaire format, but cannot be detected in the natural attributions.

Conclusions

The hypothesis of the study is, in effect, that self-reports of reasons for smoking are not robust; that is, reports of addiction are context specific rather than salient in all contexts. It is predicted that a change of context will produce a shift in the criterion for reporting addiction, and that consequently the reasons offered by smokers will vary across contexts in ways that are predictable from attribution theory. The data on contexts show that such an effect occurred with the questionnaire data. The study thus provides evidence at a FIRST (contextual) level that changing context can change verbal reports. The hypothesis is thus confirmed at this level by the questionnaire data.

However, the strongest confirmation of the hypothesis requires that the finding of "non-robustness" across contexts be supported at a SECOND level, that of method of elicitation. In other words, there should not be an interaction. To that end, the FIRST level effect, showing reports to be non-robust (variable) across contexts, should be maintained at the SECOND level; namely it should emerge regardless of which method is used. This is not the case. Whilst we have been able to demonstrate a criterion shift, this is specific to the questionnaire, and may well be due to the strength of certain signals sent by the questionnaire but not by the open-ended interview. Retrospectively, we note that the questionnaire consists of a number of items that are highly prescriptive in nature, and of a construction that would prob- ably never occur in any natural piece of conversation. On the other hand, no comparable differences emerge from the natural attributions. Consequently, the theory is confirmed at the first level but not at the second. This implies that the theory, whilst capable of producing demonstrable effects, is relatively unim- portant; or alternatively that the methodology surrounding the analysis of natural discourse is insufficiently developed. What- ever the case, the data thus provide only partial support for the theory. [Since in fact the natural attributions did not produce results contradictory to the hypothesis, but only a mish-mash of different and inconsistent themes when analysed for content in a traditional way, we prefer to assume that the fault lies in the inadequacy of methods for analysing such material, rather than in any fundamental fault in the theory – see Potter and Edwards for other examples of how authors qualify their theories every time there is a failure to replicate – nothing ever gets refuted, which might come as a surprise to Karl Popper.]

Summary of Social Criterion Theory

From the above example, we can see that verbal reports may confirm a hypothesis at: a) levels one and two, or b) at level one or two (which have quite different implications in terms of criterion and signal strength) or c) at neither level one or two. It remains only to say that social criterion theory, a crude analogy with signal detection theory, provides an overall structure for an entire data collection exercise, including a framework around which to hang the design of the study, the choice of methods to be used, and the subsequent analysis and interpretation of results.

Whilst the proposed method is perhaps overly mechanistic for some tastes, it makes no assumption that its subject matter (verbal reports) requires to meet any real or assumed logical positivist requirements in terms of semantic reference. It represents simply a principled means of dealing with data which are derived from personal experience and phenomenology, and which change according to how people construe the advantages, threats and opportunities of different situations they find themselves in. There is no implication that "good" answers are "truthful" and no requirement that they should be. Furthermore, the method can be used independent of whatever assumptions the researcher wishes to make about the links between verbal report and behaviour. All the researcher has to do is accept that people say different things in different contexts, and experience the feeling that it is high time this obvious fact was taken on board instead of being repressed.

Whilst the conception of criterion is basically the central concept in understanding verbal reports within the proposed theory, the idea of signal strength is almost equally important. This is conceptualised as a measure of the researcher's motivation, and it is argued that such a measure should now become a central requirement for all social research. If we reject, along with Koch and others (see chapter 1) the idea of the dispassionate scientist with no goals, desires of preferences of her/his own, and instead wholeheartedly embrace the concept of the scientist as a participant in a reflexive dance from which useful knowledge might emerge, the need for such a measure becomes obvious. It its absence, whole areas of "knowledge" might conceivably derive primarily from the desire of psychologists and others to find evidence to support an acceptable story that everyone wants to hear. Acceptable and largely middle-class self-delusions supported by data that have the veneer of scientific credibility do not make a sound basis for public policy.

In place of "measurement" in a traditional sense, data from studies conducted according to the above model would be evaluated in terms of their "robustness". "Robustness" indicates resistance to change under varying conditions of context and method. Thus, robust data will remain untransformed by changes in criterion or signal strength, whilst findings that are sensitive to such changes will be less robust, and the less willing one would be to generalise from them. For example, verbal reports of low self-esteem amongst teenagers who smoke, which emerge from interviews with a psychologist, with peers in a disco, from forced-choice question-naires and from open-ended discussions, might be assumed to be robust (assuming that the researcher had adequately distin-guished between the realistic appraisal of one's opportunities and likely future, and something called "low self-esteem"; that he/she has not simply labelled any self-directed comment that is other than egocentric and optimistic as "low self esteem"). Given such a broad basis, one would be prepared perhaps to make statements about low-self esteem amongst teenage smokers. On the other hand, if the only data one had came from a forced-choice questionnaire devised by an adult non-smoking psychologist (who perhaps doesn't like smoking, and can only assume that people smoke for negative reasons) and adminis-tered to samples of youngsters in a classroom, one would be more inclined to doubt their robustness and hopefully more reticent about making general statements on that very narrow basis.

Finally, the method transfers the emphasis from specific sets of verbal statements made in circumstances which are assumed to be criterion free, to the observation and analysis of the *variability* of verbal reports under a variety of conditions. It is the hope that, if verbal report does relate in any principled way to behaviour, then its actual variability may be the basis from which we should attempt to predict. It is not unreasonable to speculate that better prediction might result if we take more samples of the thing we wish to predict from, rather than hanging everything on a single example.

6

Modelling
Drugspeak

In the preceding chapters, a method was outlined which offered an integrative framework for dealing with verbal reports of all kinds. By way of illustration, an example was given of a study by McAllister and Davies which represented one of our earliest attempts to make use of the basic two-methods-two-contexts paradigm. At the end of the day, the findings were equivocal, with support for the attributional theory emerging from comparison of the contexts, but being specific to a method which sent a strong signal and undetectable in minimally cued natural explanations. The point was made that this failure could derive from a weak theory, or from lack of a strong and replicable framework for dealing with natural discourses. The next logical step, therefore, is to examine in more detail the nature of minimally cued and natural discourses with a view to finding ways of improving on our previous performance in that domain.

The first striking feature to emerge is that a common philosophy for dealing both with highly cued, highly specified data collection procedures *and* with uncued or naturalistic discourse, on the other hand, is hard to find. The distinction between the two approaches is reflected in the qualitative/quantitative dichotomy, but these two approaches are underlaid by conflicting and in some ways irreconcilable philosophical assumptions about the nature of language (see Davies 1996 *op. cit.*). In the previous chapter, however, a theory of Social Criterion was suggested which could bring both types of data into a common fold. The principle problem is that whilst psychology and other social science courses tend to offer many and manifold examples of ways of constructing and analysing questionnaire data (including such time-honoured and ubiquitous techniques as Likert, Thurstone, and Guttman scaling methods, and techniques such as semantic differential, own-categories, Q-sort, and personal constructs), no such broad menu exists for the principled and replicable analysis of less or un-structured data, beyond loose procedures such as content analysis, and qualitative techniques which have different underpinnings. Yet the Social Criterion idea assumes the equal availability of a range of methods on a continuum from highly cued to virtually uncued within a single philosophical space. It appears that one end of this continuum is rather more highly developed than the other.

Certain things seemed fairly clear at the commencement of this exercise. Firstly, we believed that commonalities in terms of motivation did in fact exist, but had so far merely eluded description in the context of minimally cued data. This implied the need for a method which would enable the testing of hypotheses, and the comparison of data from different subject groups, within a basically discursive paradigm; such a method by definition had to avoid the unacceptable face of forced-choice questionnaire-bashing and some of the more arbitrary assumptions behind quantitative methods and "measurement". On the other hand, the qualitative route was underlaid by a philosophy of discourse fundamentally at variance with that underlying quantitative methods, placing emphasis on intuitive explorations of meaning localised within context. Consequently the currently popular expedient of simply cobbling the two together as if there were no problem with doing two basically incompatible things no longer offered a graceful or pleasing solution. Indeed, in the event that different results are obtained, the problem of which is "true" remains unanswerable without resort to plausible but untestable *post hoc* rationalisations (see Davies, 1996 *op. cit.* for a discussion of these issues). The task of developing structured and replicable methods of dealing with natural discourses might therefore seem in principle impossible, since any such approach would involve forcing data into preconceived frameworks, suppress individual variation and fly in the face of the contextually-bound view of language inherent in theories of discourse. We believe however that a way forward is possible that enables the testing of conventional research hypotheses, whilst limiting the violence done to the notion of language as individually performative and contextually bound discourse, by the simple expedient of assuming all verbal reports to be motivated regardless of methods used to elicit them.

Notwithstanding some impressive philosophical counter arguments, the current chapter gives an account of an attempt to develop such a system, and presents a description of the natural history of drugspeak, based on examination of 548 minimally cued conversations with drug users at various points in their drug use careers, carried out over the last two years. The model is justified philosophically on the grounds that no reference is made to 'truth' or what the subjects' utterances "really mean"; and furthermore the status of our interpretations of what is said requires no finality. The approach is based in the philosophy of 'pragmatism' (see for example, Dewey, 1933; Mead, 1932), from which standpoint ideas are useful insofar as they help to solve problems or perform functions (to be more precise, ideas can only be evaluated in terms of their effectiveness), rather than because of their "truth" as opposed to their "falsity". By totally abandoning the search for the "truth" or the "real meaning" assumed to reside within any utterance, and concentrating entirely on the functions the utterance performs or is intended to perform in a given context, we believe that most of the objections of the discourse theory/analytic approach can be met. From such a standpoint, there is no possibility of seeking to impose a supposedly context-free, external, or definitive version of truth on any piece of discourse.

The proposed model

The model is a "process" model, and therefore invites immediate comparison with the formulations of Prochaska and DeClementi (1982, 1986) whose work of modelling the "stages of change" has proved so influential in many circles. In fact, similarities between our own model and the "stages of change" model(s), are more apparent than real. The fact that the two models "obviously" invite comparison is probably more to do with a shortage of practical and usable models of natural processes of change than anything else.

There are a number of fundamental respects in which the two models differ. The most important difference is that the functional discursive stage model described here takes as its philosophical basis the arguments expounded in the earlier chapters of this book. Thus, whilst a person who provides verbal responses that place them in, say, the 'contemplation' stage of the Prochaska and DeClementi model is assumed to be "really" describing an "internal state" that they are "in", no such assumption is required in the proposed discursive stage model. Instead of the driving force for the discourse being a person's attempts to describe their own internal processes, a problem fraught with philosophical difficulties as noted in chapter 3, the different species of natural discourse identified by the discursive stage model are assumed to emerge in predictable and orderly form by virtue of the contexts within which particular types of drug use take place. To the extent that there are repeated conjunctions of certain types of context and certain drug-related behaviours, consensual acts of discourse will emerge; not because they are inherently "true", but because they make functional sense to large numbers of people who use drugs and are in broadly the same situation.

Since these contexts are culturally determined, involving public perceptions and responses to drug use, certain legal sanctions, the conceptualisation of drug use by social workers, addiction agencies, the press and media and so forth, there is nothing absolute about these discourses. They are culturally relative, since the culture creates the contexts in which drug use takes place. As with the notion of psychophysical threshold, therefore, there is no issue to discuss with respect to whether the verbal reports themselves are "true" or not, or whether they represent anything "real". Finally, it follows that the natural history of drug discourse is not a natural history in any broad sense (i.e. a global theory) but will emerge differently from cultures which create different contexts for their drug users. Unfortunately, data on this issue are scarce and hard to obtain, a problem which is likely to become more rather than less acute as Western influence spreads.

In short, therefore, Prochaska and DiClementi assume that any consistency in verbal reports from drug users arises because they are in the same internal state. The discursive stage model assumes any such consistency arises because they are in the same external situation. It just so happens that, sometimes, telling people you are in a particular state is the best thing to do in that situation.

A functional framework for "Drugspeak"

The development of a framework for classifying conversations with drug users followed loosely from the kinds of procedures for dealing with qualitative data suggested by Miles and Huberman (1984), giving particular attention to the types of methods outlined in chapters 2 and 3 of that text. On the basis of minimally cued natural conversations with opportunity samples of drug users, a conceptual framework emerged. This emerged from notes, transcriptions, tape recordings and group discussions, and centred around the task of building a series of propositions about the types of conversations being encountered. These propositions however were not concerned with the surface content of the conversations but with underlying functional attributional dimensions of the type referred to in previous work (Davies, 1992.) It will be recalled that previous work by McAllister and Davies (*op. cit.*) had made use of dimensions derived from Weiner, and included stability, locus, and controllability; and that these had failed to produce meaningful patterns of prediction when applied to natural discourse. From the outset, therefore, it was clear that those dimensions, or even those *kinds* of dimensions, would not prove helpful in the present context.

A number of schemes were suggested of varying degrees of complexity, until the emergence of the scheme that is now described in the following pages. This is by no means necessarily the best scheme, and we fully expect there will be changes and modifications in the future. It simply represents the best scheme we have come up with so far that meets criteria in terms of a) discrimination and prediction and b) inter-rater replicability.

A Functional-Discursive Model of "Drugspeak"

In this study (Davies 1997), interviews were carried out with problem drug and alcohol users in South Ayrshire, Glasgow, Lothian and in Newcastle-upon-Tyne. Initial (first) interviews were carried out with 275 subjects; subsequently, second interviews were carried out with 197 of these; and third interviews were carried out with 76 of the original sample. Using the first interview as a baseline, the drop-out rate using the methodology described was thus high, particularly at the third interview; namely 28% at second interview, and 72% at third interview. The study was of two years' duration, with the interval between interviews varying between 3 and 6 months. Interviews were conducted in a variety of locations, sometimes in treatment centres, sometimes in the subjects' own homes, and sometimes elsewhere but always subject to the preference of the interviewee. The interviews were conducted by casually dressed and informal interviewers with no formal connections with any treatment agency.

The interviews were confidential, but not anonymous, since it was necessary to retain confidential ID information in order to arrange follow-ups. All interviews were tape-recorded, and subsequently transcribed. In the process, 60 interviews were carried out which were subsequently unusable, due to inaudibility, unintelligibility, or a breakdown in the interview. The numbers given in the above paragraph are the numbers of usable transcripts actually obtained.

The interviews were of fairly short duration ranging from 10 to 20 minutes, with a median of about 15 minutes. All interviews were minimally cued. There was no set procedure, and no set of issues which "had to be covered". Consequently, it was hoped that the issues raised in the conversations would be ones which were of salience to the subject and not the researcher; that is, the researcher's signal strength would be low.

After initial pleasantries, all interviews commenced in the same manner with the question,

"So what are you on, what are you using at the moment?",

or some linguistic variant on that formula. Interviewees would then describe the present state of their habit. Thereafter, interviewers were merely instructed to explore reasons for use in order to obtain as many natural attributions as possible and to seek clarification of things that were not clear. There was no pre-formulated structure to the interview, and no set of key issues or questions that had to be addressed. In short, therefore, if subjects didn't spontaneously tell us about it, we didn't find out about it.

During pilot interviews, durations of up to and even exceeding one hour were experienced. It was therefore decided that all interviews should be restricted to fifteen minutes, for two reasons. Firstly, on the basis of preliminary discussions we inclined to the view that the most salient reasons would emerge early rather than late. This is an assumption. We are aware that others would take the view that deeper and more important information often emerges later (e.g. Orford: personal communication) but this was not the view taken here. We cannot comment on the idea that "truth" takes a longer rather than a shorter time to emerge, for reasons discussed in earlier chapters. A functional theory of drugspeak of the type postulated here requires that discourse be functional from the outset; we cannot envisage a rationale for subjects "holding back" functional accounts till later in an interview, and we struggle with the problem of what is a non-functional account. Whether they might hold back "true" answers is outside the remit of this theory. Secondly, practical experience suggested that given unlimited time, subjects would produce and rehearse a vast range of reasons and types of attribution for their drug use, which complicated rather than clarified the situation. We assumed therefore that the strongest (most functional) internal signals ought to produce a functional account earlier rather than later in any conversation and that subsequent confirmation or disconfirmation of the theory would take place in the light of that assumption.

The aim was to examine the transcripts and to devise a classification system into which all future transcripts would fit. We are fully aware that within the theory and philosophy of discourse analysis such procedures are generally viewed as doing violence to personal and localised meanings and as representing one of the ways in which standard research methodologies suppress individual variability. However, we felt justified in taking this step provided any system we devised was derived from a theory concerning underlying functional dimensions rather than attempting to code "actual meaning". The latter course is not valid within a discursive theory, since the researcher's interpretation of what any such meaning "actually" is cannot be sustained, as discussed in earlier chapters. Furthermore, there is no assumption here that such a functional system represents some higher order "truth", nor that "truth" inheres either in the transcripts or in our interpretation of them. The result, we hope, is a functional typology of "drugspeak" which is largely independent of the surface or apparent semantic meaning of what is said. The drugspeak model is merely intended to be empirically useful insofar as it links conversations, which are classified according to type rather than content, with particular activities which characterise different stages of progress through a drug-using career.

In brief, the aim is to provide an answer to two questions, namely a) *"What kind of conversation is this?"* such that different people who read a transcript can agree as to its type with a high degree of consensus; and b) given that there is agreement about the type of conversation, *"Is there anything useful we can predict*

from that?". Note that the prediction is independent of any assumptions about truth or falsity, and derives from an *a priori* typology
into which it is assumed all conversations can fit rather than
from a normal discourse analysis in which "themes" are identified *ex post facto* which characterise that particular piece of text.

The model, first described by Davies (1996), places conversations
with substance users into one of six boxes, each of which has
certain characteristics. At the time of writing, the system is
characterised by redundancy in the sense that there are more
characteristics than are necessary in order to make a unique
assignment; assignment is thus overdetermined. However, analysis
suggests ways in which the number of predictors might be reduced
(see next chapter) in the context of future studies. The basic
form of the model is illustrated in Figure 2 below.

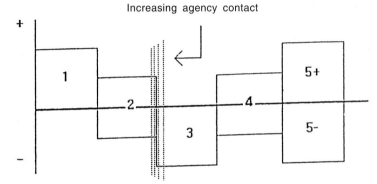

Figure 2. Five-stage discursive model of the addiction process.
(N.B. Movement from box 3 to box 2 is not possible within this model)

The horizontal axis represents the passage of time, so a complete
discursive "cycle" is depicted, from non-addicted use, through
an addictive-discourse stage, and finally to a resolution or outcome
stage. The vertical axis represents an `addiction' dimension which
at the time of writing has only 2 states (addicted and non-addicted).
We have conceptualised this in evaluative terms (plus and minus)
since it makes the model easier to talk about. Thus events above
the line are seen as non-addicted and therefore `positive', whilst
events below the line are seen as addicted and therefore negative.
The logical basis for this goes no further than the assumption
that `addiction' is seen as the thing to be changed, and `non-
addiction' as the desired outcome condition. It is not possible to
cycle round the whole model more than once, though we would
wish to identify a number of subcycles which are possible within

the model. Viewing the model as a whole, it represents a "life-course", in the sense that one proceeds from left to right over the course of a life time, subject to some subcycling between adjacent boxes. There is no guarantee however that one will eventually arrive in either of the stage-5 boxes (we believe that some users spend large periods of their lives cycling around boxes 3 and 4). There is one other constraint which is theoretically derived. Once a person has arrived at stage 3, it is impossible to return to the earlier stages (1 and 2) of the model, since once a type-3 "addicted" discourse has been adopted, it is impossible to become the type of person who had never adopted it, and vestiges of that discourse persist into box 5 positive.

It is easiest to conceptualise the boxes which comprise the model in intuitive terms before proceeding to the level of the dimensions which we think identify the boxes. The reader is reminded, if such is necessary, that the model does not represent stages a person is 'in', but merely a number of identifiable types of conversations it is possible to have with drug users. If at various points in this text we talk about people being 'in' a particular box, we imply no internal state; merely that they produced a particular type of discourse. The model is entirely discursive. It makes no assumptions about whether or not people are reporting on various internal 'states'; nor does it require decisions about whether a particular piece of discourse is true or false.

Six types of "drugspeak"

Box 1 is basically a type of conversation which characterises drug use as positive, fun, problem free, and as having no negative consequences for health, social or economic functioning. This is the stage of hedonistic recreational drug use. There is no suggestion of dependent use or "addiction" and the conversation in its most clear form will be enthusiastic about drug use. No problems will be reported as arising from the use. No attempt will be made to explain any past or existing life problems (of whatever nature) as consequences of drug use; nor will drug use be described as a response to such life problems. Any consequences of drug use will be described in humorous terms rather than in problem-language. Typically, type 1 discourse comes from younger drug users taking recreational drugs such as ecstasy, amphetamines,

LSD, or alcohol, and the context for drug use will often be the disco, the rave, or the pub. It is not, however, restricted to that age group nor that range of situations; we have encountered type 1 discourse from heroin users in their 30s. Finally, type 1 discourse is stable and uncontradictory over a wide range of situations and circumstances.

Box 2 represents a type of discourse which is unstable and contradictory. The discourse alternates between a generally positive view of drug use resembling type 1, and a generally negative style, according to the function of the conversation at that time. Type 2 discourse emerges from type 1 when problems begin to arise from drug use which cannot be ignored, either because of their magnitude or the context in which they occur. These problems can be of any kind, subject to the requirement that pressure is placed on the individual to explain his/her drug use to an outside agency or third party (e.g. teacher, parent, police, social work, doctor). The person now is required to continue presenting a hedonistic and volitional view of drug use in order to maintain their position within their present peer group, but also increasingly to adopt a more negative and more problem oriented type of discourse for disapproving others. This is a critical box, since at this point the person has to decide whether to proceed to box 3 (often by deciding to seek agency contact) or to reimpose control and return to box 1. The pressures will typically be towards box 3.

Box 3 is the "addicted" box. Discourse of this type makes open reference to loss of volition and control. Any reference to hedonism or enjoyment is lost, and is replaced instead by negative statements about the consequences of drug use. The language of AA is an archetypal box 3 discourse but it is by no means the only one. Furthermore, box 3 discourse places drug use in a context that makes such use seem logical or inevitable. Thus, drug use will be described as an inevitable outcome of certain physiological or constitutional factors over which the individual has no control, and which have existed over a period of time; or as a forced consequence of negative life events and situations which again have a history. Box 3 discourse is consistent and invariant over context. Most people employing box 3 discourse will in fact be in full agency contact, or moving into such agency contact. Our data suggest that type 3 discourse may in some sense be a prerequisite for agency contact, since those who entered full agency contact during the course of the study were employing type 3 discourse prior to such involvement.

Box 4 discourse resembles box 2 in being contradictory and context dependent. Box 4 discourse represents the stage at which the 'addiction' concept starts to break down either temporarily or fundamentally, for the individual concerned. The inconsistency stems from a tension between the requirements of the addict role as exemplified in box 3, and a recurring discontent with those requirements. Thus, while still endorsing the addict stereotype, the box 4 user will also produce reports that drug use can be a positive experience, and that it does not necessarily lead to negative consequences. This is the stage when lapse or relapse occurs (or is "made to occur" – see Christo 1995. Christo's data suggest that relapses may often be "planned" in advance, rather than being manifestations of some monolithic and inevitable process) the outcome of such lapse or relapse being either a return to box 3, or a move into one of the '5' boxes.

Box 5 positive we have labelled "up and out", and according to this model represents the best outcome for any person who has entered box 3. Whilst 5 positive discourse still contains reference to addiction, such reference will be in the past. Both the addiction, and the reasons for it, will be viewed as "over and done with". The person accepts that they had a serious problem, but they have left it behind. Consequently, their current state (they may be abstinent or using again in a non-problematic way) is not based on any requirement to see themselves as "a recovering addict". In an interview with the saxophone player Art Pepper, (The Late Shift; Notes of a Jazz Survivor; ITV circa 1986; in the author's possession) Pepper openly concedes that he has been a heroin addict, and has committed a variety of crimes including armed robbery in order to support the habit. He says *"But I'm a genius. I don't hear anyone doing anything as good as me."* He takes out a chocolate bar, and says, *"Sweets. This is the toughest. This is one I could never kick."* The addiction is thus in the past, the present lifestyle has a new positive focus and is not predicated on any need to guard indefinitely against the reinstatement of addiction, and he can make jokes about addiction. On returning to his former haunts, he comments, *"God... I'd love to get high"* but he does not do so.

Box 5 negative we have called "down and out". This is the box containing those who have failed the system, and/or whom the system has failed. Five negative is a kind of limbo in which a person is parked permanently, until such time as he/she can persuade an agency to take them on again, or otherwise gain access to some social support or treatment agency. They will normally have `failed' a number of agency contacts; they may be living on the streets; they are probably inebriated and/or dysfunctional for long periods. Any discourse obtained is rambling and incoherent. We have failed to obtain usable transcripts of 5 negative in any numbers that make meaningful analysis possible. Therefore, the main characteristic (at the time of writing) is this lack of meaningful structure or content in terms of the proposed system. The only samples we have are extremely brief, and highly dismissive.

Usability/replicability of the system

The categorisation system described above and in Fig. 2 is derived in the first instance from examination of transcripts, tapes and notes. To provide some initial evidence that such a system might be usable in a reliable way by different researchers, and in principle communicable to others, 20 transcripts were randomly selected from the pool available at an early stage of the research. These were then coded in accordance with the above descriptive system by four research workers who had been involved in the data collection and in the development of the category scheme

Table 1

	J	M	D	F	Consensus
Billy	1	1	1	1	4/4
Michelle	1	1	1	1	4/4
Tam	1	1	1	1	4/4
Anthony	4	4	4	3 (4)	3/4
Peter	3	3	3	3	4/4
Dianne	4	4	3 (4)	3	2 = 2
Steven	1	1	1	1	4/4
Ian	1	1	1	1	4/4
Brian	2	2	2	2	4/4
John	4	4	4	4	4/4
Alan	5 –	4	4	3	
Mark	3	4	3	3	3/4
John	2	2	2	2	4/4
Flora	2	4	4	4	3/4
Patricia	3	3	3	3	4/4
John	4	3	3	4	2 = 2
Mark	2	1	2	2	3/4
Donna	4	5+	4	+5 (4)	2 = 2
Thomas	5 +	4	5+	5+	3/4
Paul	2	2	2	1	3/4

Of 20 transcripts :	All four agree	10
	Three in one box	6
	Two in one, two in another	3
	Complete disagreement	1

(J. Davies, D. Best, F. McConnochie & M. Crugeira). Table 1 above shows the results of this exercise. The 20 subjects are listed vertically, and the stages to which they were assigned by each of the four judges are listed in the adjacent columns. The degree of consensus is given in the final column.

Given that there are six possible categories of assignment; and under a (false) assumption of equiprobability* of occurrence; the chances of all four judges agreeing on any one box, given that judge 1 has already assigned subject x to box y, are 6 to the power 3, or 216 to 1. As can be seen from the table, there is an encouraging degree of consensus. There is total agreement on ten transcripts. Three out of four judges agree on a further 6 transcripts. Finally, on nine of the ten transcripts over which there is less than perfect agreement, the disagreement over assignment involves only one box, usually some uncertainty between boxes 3 and 4. In one case (Flora) there is a fundamental disagreement, involving the pre-addiction (boxes 1 and 2) and post-addiction (boxes 3, 4 and 5) phases of the model.

The data in Table 2 suggested to us that in principle the system might be workable, and that given further development it should be possible to achieve a high degree of consensus between judges making intuitive judgements, using nothing more that the descriptions of the stages provided in the previous section. There is clearly therefore some *phenomenological reality* about the kinds of drug discourses described.

However, the degree of consensus achieved involved four judges who were intimately involved in both the data collection and the production of the typology, and who were consequently very much in touch with each other's thinking. Informal attempts to describe the system and teach it to others in the context of workshop seminars at the Universities of Leeds and Canterbury (during 1995) did not produce such high degrees of correspondence, but did produce a number of comments and cogent objection. It was clear that the system as described did not provide a comprehensive account of how the four researchers carried out the task and that

---

*The data clearly suggest that some discourses may be more frequent than others. However, at this stage we do not possess normative data from a population sample on the basis of which to give reasonably precise probability estimates. It seems likely, however, that either category of 5 is a rare event; 5 positive because many subjects appear to get caught up in a repeated 3/4/3/4 subcycle; and 5 negative due to difficulties of obtaining and making sense of data from that group.

those intimately concerned with the project were taking certain things for granted, ignoring certain contrary information, and in other ways using prior experience in the production of their ratings. It was clear that substantial work was required if the system was to become communicable to, and usable in a consistent way by, other workers.

Dimensions and rating scales

As a result of further discussions of tapes, notes, and other material, the researchers involved in the project devised a second-order framework for the classification of drug discourses. Previous work was also taken into account, including attribution research by Davies *et al.*, work by Crugeira who was working on the same problem in Portugal for her Ph.D., and Best, also working for a Ph.D. in the area of discourse analysis. Crugeira had initially shown the limitations of the Kelley and Weiner-type dimensions in this area, and Best was basically opposed to standard attributional measures on philosophical grounds.

Working as a team we devised an overdetermined system for the classification of discourses, using as its basis *the things we thought we might be basing our judgements on*. We produced a system involving seven descriptive dimensions. These included some which we believe are original in this area as well as others which clearly bear some relationship to previous attributional dimensions. The dimensions were *time, generalisability, purposiveness, hedonism, reductionism, contradictoriness*, and *addicted self-ascription*. On the basis of our discussions, we then deductively derived the scheme

Table 2.

	STAGE					
	1	2	3	4	5+	5 –
TIME	Pr	M	P	M	Pr	P
GENERALISABILITY	Lo	M	Hi	M	Lo	M
PURPOSIVENESS	Hi	M	Lo	M	Hi	Lo
HEDONISM	Hi	M	Lo	M	M/Hi	Lo
REDUCTIONISM	Psy	M	Soc/Phy	M	Psy	?
CONTRADICTORINESS	Ab	Pr	Ab	Pr	Ab	Ab
ADDICTED SELF-ASCRIPTION	Ab	Ab	Pr	Pr	Ab	Ab

* Key : Pr = Present, M = Mixed, P = Past, Hi = High, Lo = Low, Psy = Psychological, Soc = Social, Phy = Physiological, Ab = Absent. Note that under the 'time' dimension, the term 'present' implies the opposite of 'past'. Under the dimensions of 'contradictoriness' and 'addicted self-ascription', the term 'present' implies the opposite of 'absent'.

outlined in Table 2 above, in which we suggest the ways in which the patterning of these seven dimensions should be distributed over the discursive stages.

The dimensions are assumed to be underlying dimensions within the transcripts. They characterise the *reasons* which are given for drug use, and not *the drug use itself*. This distinction is crucial. Early confusions and failures with this system arose due to the tendency to code the drug use in terms of the dimensions, rather than the reasons for that use.

The TIME dimension was the most easily confused. Time is coded as 'past' if current drug use is attributed to reasons that lie in the past. For example, if current use is attributed to break up of a past relationship ("My wife left me five years ago"), the text is characterised as 'past'. Concurrent reasons are coded as 'present' ("My man uses and I feel I might as well join him"). Note that reports about drug-use history ("I started using about ten years ago") do not enable coding in the time dimension, which must derive from the *reasons* for use. If the text as a whole cannot be reasonably characterised in either of these terms, it is assigned to the 'mixed' category.

GENERALISABILITY refers to a tendency to invoke a broad range of factors as being causal in connection with current drug use. Thus social, personal, employment, health, family and other factors will feature in accounts that are HI on this dimension. By contrast, drug use explained in terms of a single, or a small and focused group of factors, will be LO on generalisability. If the text overall cannot be reasonably characterised in either of these terms, it is assigned to the 'mixed' category.

PURPOSIVENESS is basically a volitional dimension. Text which makes reference to drug use as arising from wishes, desires, decisions, purposes or other terms which imply choice or decision making, is said to be HI on this dimension. By contrast, accounts which characterise the drug use as a forced or inevitable response to either internal states or external circumstances are said to be LO. If the text overall cannot reasonably be characterised in either of these ways, it is said to be 'mixed'.

HEDONISM characterises accounts where drug use is referred to in terms which have a positive evaluative and emotional tone. The experience is described as enjoyable or desirable, and these positive effects are sought after. Younger users often refer to "fun" in connection with their drug taking. In such cases, hedonism is HI. By contrast, accounts, which have no such positive tone, or refer explicitly to lack of any pleasure are LO on hedonism. Contradictory accounts are `mixed'.

REDUCTIONISM is an attempt to code the type or 'flavour' of the accounts. It does not simply overlap PURPOSIVENESS. We struggled with this dimension on a number of occasions, and further development is clearly necessary. At the time of this preliminary analysis, each transcript was coded in terms of psychological (PSY), physical/physiological (PHYS) or social (SOC) types of reductionism. Within any transcript, one, two, or all three of these may occur. We thus coded reductionism in terms of the presence or absence of three types of explanatory framework any or all of which may be discerned in a given transcript.

CONTRADICTORINESS refers to any or all of the dimensions above, and refers to the tendency to provide explanatory accounts that are mutually exclusive at different points in the interview, as opposed to a more internally consistent account. What this points to is a highly localised and unstable pattern of functionality which is sensitive to particular issues within the conversation. It is an assumption of this model that such instability within a transcript would correlate with lack of consistency between contexts outwith that conversation; consequently we see this as a putative index of a more broadly based contextually cued variability of the type documented by Ball (1967) and by Davies and Baker (1987). Contradictoriness is coded as absent/present.

ADDICTED SELF-ASCRIPTION refers to the tendency to explain drug use in terms of a general 'addiction' stereotype. Initially, we restricted this to the actual use of the word 'addiction' or 'addict', but this was subsequently broadened to include any 'addicted' type of discourse even if the specific word was not used. This dimension is inductively not independent of the other dimensions, and is something of a catch-all. This is again simply coded as absent/present.

A coding sheet was devised on which the self-reports of drug use were rated (see Figure 3). This involved an attempt to assess present extent of drug use from the transcripts (see next chapter), followed by a series of scales for the rating of the seven dimensions. By relating the data from these seven subscales to the final discursive stage to which a given transcript was allocated, we hoped to shed light on the manner in which we were using the system. By so doing, we hoped to make the system more communicable to others, since we would be in a position to identify those dimensions which were central to, or peripheral to, decisions about which

CODING MECHANISM

1) ID :

2)

3) LOCATION :   SEX

                                               AMOUNT

4) PRESCRIBED DRUG USE :   i)   METHADONE

                                   ii)   DIAZEPAM

                                  iii)   TEMAZEPAM

                                  iv)   OTHER

                                            FREQUENCY

5) STREET DRUG USE :   i)   HEROIN

                                 ii)   METHADONE

                                 iii)   TEMAZEPAM

                                 iv)   DIAZEPAM

                                 v)   ECSTASY

                                 vi)   LSD

                                vii)   SPEED

                               viii)   COCAINE

                                ix)   CANNABIS

                                x)   ALCOHOL

                                xi)   SOLVENTS

                                xii)   OTHER

6) INJECTION :

7) OVERALL ASSESSMENT :

                                             Circle the appropriate number

8) PURPOSIVENESS:

	1	2	3	4	5
	HI				LO

9) HEDONISM:

	1	2	3	4	5
	HI				LO

10) GENERALISABILITY

	1	2	3	4	5
	HI				LO

11) TIME:

	1	2	3	4	5
	PRESENT				PAST

                                   Tick beneath all that are appropriate

12) REDUCTIONISM:

         PSYCHOLOGICAL   PHYSIOLOGICAL   SOCIOLOGICAL

13) ADDICTION:

14) CONTRADICTORINESS:

15) STAGE:

16) What stage do you predict this subject will be in at next interview:

Figure 3. Coding sheets for analysis of discourse.

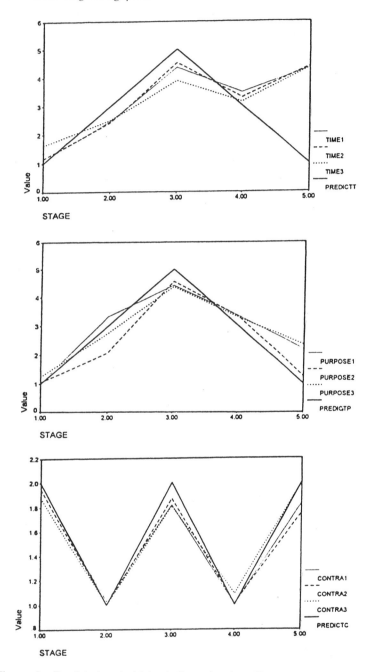

Figure 4. Predicted and obtained dimensional profiles.

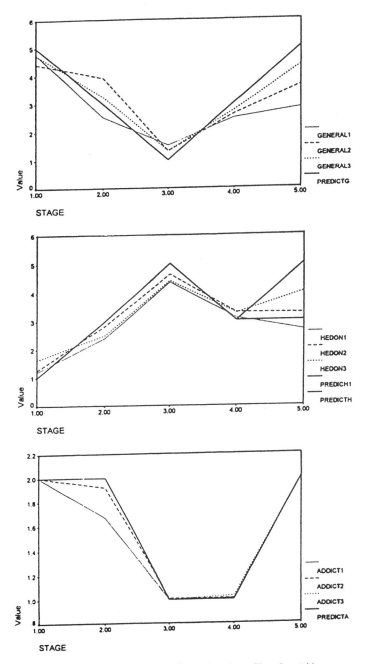

Figure 4. Predicted and obtained dimensional profiles (contd.)

stage a particular discourse belonged to.

The analysis of these data commenced with the production of a series of graphs or profiles comparing the deductive predictions of the model provided in Table 2, with the actual mean scores obtained for the various dimensions. The deductive model is validated against the empirical data by examining the agreement between the contour-profile of the two curves. The solid line represents the predicted pattern; the dotted lines describe the way in which decisions about stages were actually made. Graphs for each dimension, based on independent data collected at first, second and third interviews, are shown. Due to the Likert scoring system, a value of 1 represents a high (HI) level of hedonism, generalisability and purposiveness, with 5 representing the low (LO) end of the dimension. For addicted self-ascription and contradictoriness, 1 equals 'present' and 2 equals 'absent'. For time 1 equals 'time present' and 5 equals 'time past'. Inspection shows a reasonable degree of agreement between coding at all three interviews, and also with the predicted pattern. The graphs appear in Figure 4.

Three points require some comment. Firstly, visual inspection shows a reasonable fit between the data from different interviews, and the predicted profile reflects the obtained profiles for the most part. It is notable however that the 'time' dimension does not fit the predicted pattern for stage 5. The researchers predicted a return to 'time present', resembling stage 1, for those who achieve stage 5 discourse, but this was not the case. There were still strong elements of 'time past' in stage 5 which were not anticipated. Secondly, our initial discussions were unable to resolve the issue of whether stage 5 discourse would return to full hedonism, and so we have represented this state of affairs in terms of a prediction pattern which branches at stage 4. In the event, hedonism at stage 5, whilst clearly above that for stage 3, remains somewhat variable in stage 5. Finally, no graphical data are presented for reductionism. This latter dimension, it will be recalled, was coded in terms of three types of reductionism (physical, social, psychological) and does not lend itself to graphical representation. As will be shown later, this dimension adds little to overall prediction.

It is important that the reader places an appropriate interpretation upon these data. We may in a sense conceptualise the judges' rating forms as a type of "questionnaire about a transcript". In effect the task of each rater was equivalent to an instruction to "read this transcript and then fill in the following questionnaire about it". The graphs described above show systematic variability in the ways the rating scales were used and the overall discursive stage to which subjects were assigned. In traditional social cognitive models, the discovery of patterns of association between subsets of items, one of which is assumed to be an independent variable for the purposes of analysis, are often taken to indicate causal relationships between psychological entities. Perhaps the archetypal model of this type is the Fishbein and Ajzen (1975) model. In this and subsequent models, answers to sets of questions intended to "measure" (assumed) independent entities such as subjective norms, objective norms, attitudes, beliefs and so forth are subsequently found to correlate with each other in certain ways when the data are analysed. Within such a social cognitive framework the conceptualisation of subsets of items as measuring independent entities which then have a causal connection is central to the interpretation of the data. In the present case, however, such a conceptualisation must be deemed inappropriate.

From a discursive point of view, as we have seen in an earlier chapter, it is argued that there are no entities in the brain. Since we sympathise with, or at least have an open mind on, this issue, then the idea that such entities are "measured" by our procedures must be treated with some caution within the theoretical context of the present study. Consequently, what we would suggest is that the above data merely show that the same "story" or "script" is tapped by different methods. Similarly with models such as Fishbein and Ajzen (*op. cit.*) we would argue that patterns of correlations arise not because there is a causal connection between psychological entities but merely because different subsets of questions tap basically the same deep script or story. The above data therefore should not be interpreted within a social cognitive framework. Nothing has been "discovered" that was not there before, and no pattern of causal connections has been revealed between independent entities.

The graphical data should be interpreted therefore in the light of the chapter on signal detection theory. We have asked some judges to carry out a rating exercise on some transcripts in two different ways. On the one hand they have a holistic method based on a verbal description of the types of story they may be expected to encounter. On the other hand, there is also a method that makes use of forced-choice dimensions and rating scales such as might be employed in a standard "measurement" exercise.

The close correspondence revealed by the graphs above simply shows that the coding system devised is robust. People carry out this exercise in a reliable and predictable fashion and this is true whether they use a holistic method based on an unstructured descriptive typology of the types of stories, or a rating scale/ forced-choice method. The correct interpretation, therefore, is merely that the system devised is "robust", in principle communicable to others and remains stable under two contrasting methods. Thus whether one uses forced-choice rating scales or holistic descriptions as the basis for one's coding, we may expect with some confidence that the same types of result will be obtained.

In the light of the above, the reliability of the system was assessed in one more way, and at a more detailed level. We have already seen how four raters assigned 20 transcripts to the five-stage model, on the basis of the general intuitive stage descriptions, with a fair degree of consensus. We have also seen how assignation of transcripts to stages agreed rather well with the deductive predictions based on the hypothesised underlying dimensions. In a third reliability check, we took a further set of 47 transcripts, (this should have been 50, but one coder received three incomplete transcripts) and one of the workers who devised the system undertook to train a post-graduate student with no prior knowledge of this piece of research, in the method. Furthermore, data were collected not merely for the reliability of the stage of assignment, but also for the reliabilities of the scores on the individual Likert scales used in coding each of the underlying dimensions. The results from this final reliability examination are summarised in Table 3 below, in the form of simple agreement rates.

Table 3

Agreement Rates for Final Reliability Check, by Stage, and by each Dimension

	Same	1 dis.	2 dis.	3 dis.
Stage	33	12	2	0
Purposiveness	27	15	4	1
Hedonism	24	16	7	0
Generalisability	23	19	4	1
Time	29	11	7	0
	Same	1 omission	2 oms.	3 oms.
Reductionism	21	18	5	3

Table 3 above shows the number of total agreements and disagreements between the two coders. The disagreement columns (1 dis. etc.) show category disagreements of different widths, and the numbers obtained of each. Under 'reductionism', the 'same' column shows an identical profile obtained for 21 subjects. Disagreements indicate the number of omissions characterising each disagreed profile. Finally, data for 'contradictoriness' and for attribution of 'addiction' are not included as these are artefactually high due the combined effects of a two-point scale (present/ absent) and the fact that stage three is defined principally by 'addiction', whilst 'contradictoriness' identifies stage two or four. Thus, agreement about certain stages effectively ensures agreement about these two dimensions. The data in the table show a majority of agreed decisions on all components; with disagreement by a single scale point as the next most frequent category. For those who prefer inferential statistics, the correlations (Pearson) between coders were as follows: stage 0.90; purposiveness 0.87; hedonism 0.77; generalisability 0.83; time 0.82. (all coefficients significant at $p < 0.001$).

In concluding this section, we may therefore say that the discursive prototype for drugspeak outlined in the above chapter has phenomenological reality. Our own researchers can code drug conversation reliably, and given time and patience, others can be trained to code them in ways that produce useful levels of replicability. Secondly, agreement about the stages to which conversations are assigned is not merely skin deep or impressionistic; it arises due to principled agreement at a more detailed level as to what the defining discursive characteristics of those conversations are. In summary therefore, it can be concluded that 'drugspeak', as a form of developmental script, exists. People can use it; and others can recognise it. However, the proposal is that the consensus in types of conversations arises not because all drug users encounter the same problems, have the same experiences, and lead the same lives at certain points in their career (a suggestion which taxes the bounds of probability) but because it becomes necessary for them to invoke certain types of explanation at certain points by virtue of the social context in which their drug use takes place. If this assertion is a useful one, then the key to understanding addiction lies in disentangling the functionality (purpose) of what is said, and identifying the pressures that lead to such discourse being necessary, and ultimately to being acted out or "coming true", rather than concentrating on surface content and confronting the riddle of telling "truth" from "lies".

Consequently given that we can identify and code conversations, recognise types of story, and agree about a typology, what use is there in such an exercise if the veridical status of what is said remains unknown; indeed, unknowable according to the philosophical underpinnings of this approach? And how can the functionality of such discourses be demonstrated? In chapter 7 it is proposed to give some examples of the different types of discourses described so that the reader can form his/her opinion of the ease of application and the appropriateness of the system described above. Then in chapter 8 an attempt is made to answer the second of the two questions posed above. Namely, can any suggestions be made as to the functionality of the different types of discourses on the basis of a statistical analysis of their predictive utility?

7

Drug
Discourses

Chapter 7 presents examples of the discursive types described above. It will be remembered that discourse of type 5– was not obtained in any quantity, and tended to be extremely brief, so the most important examples cover the range of types 1,2,3,4 and 5+. A single example of type 5– is also included. This was identified under rather special circumstances which are described later in this chapter. The examples given have, obviously, been specially selected for inclusion in this text. Not all examples are easily codable in terms of the system, and notwithstanding the high reliabilities obtained between judges, ambiguities do occur. Nonetheless it is hoped that the examples will give the reader a "feel" for the processes involved. For the purposes of this exercise, names of individuals and of agencies have been changed or deleted.

Throughout the following scripts, the letter "I" refers to "interviewer" and the letter "S" refers to "interviewee" (subject).

Example of type 1 discourse

I   *So can you tell me what drugs you use at the moment?*
S.   *...speed, acid, cannabis, eh, just drink..., that's about it.*
I.   *So what makes you decide what you're going to buy?*
S.   *It all depends on the mood I'm in on the night...*
I.   *How do you mean the mood?*
S.   *Well, some nights we'll just get a drink, or if we're going out to the dancing or anything we'll take speed.*

I. *Why is that?*

S. *More energy for the night... eh, then some nights we'll just get acid, (why is that?)... we don't do it very often it's just a thing that we do sometimes.*

I. *Would you say that you're influenced by your friends sometimes?*

S. *Sometimes, but sometimes I suggest it to my friends and then...*

I. *But what makes you think "I'll do some acid tonight?"*

S. *It all depends on the night, if it's a good night it's better than getting a drink... (how do you mean if it's a good night?)... If we're having fun we'll just go and get an acid.*

I. *What about availability and money, would that influence you?*

S. *It's dead easy to get it...*

I. *So how·long have you used drugs for?*

S. *Three years, four year...*

I. *So why do you do drugs do you think?*

S. *Just started off as a night out, then somebody suggested it, then I took my first acid and enjoyed it, after that I just took it every so often, just decided that way...*

I. *But why do you use drugs?*

S. *There's nothing else to do at nights. The club's only on during the week, the weekends there's nothing much else. In (name of town) there's nothing much else do to. It's mostly boredom, it's anything that happens, if you're caught drinking all the time the police are always going for people that's drunk, so when you're on acid you still know what you're doing so...*

I. *So would you say you feel in control?*

S. *It just means I would'nae try and get addicted to them... well I know what they do to you but I still like taking them but it's very rarely that I do take one, just every so often.*

I. *Do you see yourself sort of having changed over the last few years as regards the drug taking? Have you experimented a bit more through that time or what?*

S. *Well... people always tell you that you should'nae be taking them, taking drugs and that, but to me it's just something I like doing. It's fun, it's good fun.*

I. *Have you ever encompassed (encountered) any problems at all within the last three years in association with your drug use?*

S. *No.*

I. But has anything been happening in your life that would make you decide to go out and use?

S. It all depends like, sometimes like if I'm having an argument with somebody or I've had a hard day at work I'll go out and maybe get drunk that night, but for drugs it would be something different, eh, if there's if I've had a day in work and I don't want to go out and drink, it's cheaper just to get an acid, so I'll just get an acid instead.

I. So would it depend on finances, expenses then?

S. Aye, if I'm skint I'll get an acid that night.

I. Have you ever had any agency contact?

S. Nope.

I. What about parents, family, how do they see it?

S. They don't really know I take drugs.

I. Why not do you think?

S. I've never told them, I know how they'd react, they'd be pretty angry and that...

I. So how do you see yourself? Do you see yourself as a junkie? a recreational user? How do you see it?

S. Just recreational... just whenever...I just occasionally take a drug; take something for the night, but mostly cannabis and drink.

I. Why? Do you mainly go out to get pissed or what?

S. I drive as well so sometimes when I do go out I don't drink at all.

I. But what makes you decide that you're going to go out and get pissed?

S. I just end up getting drunk, just whenever it's a good night... know (you know) we all go out and you don't realise how much you're actually drinking, it catches up with you, and before you know it you're drunk.

I. So what about your future, how do you see that? Would you want to stop doing drugs totally?

S. No because I enjoy doing it. Aye, that's it.

I. Do you think you'll be able to stop then?

S. If I wanted to stop I could.

I. So what about the future do you see yourself as maybe dabbling in different types of drugs out of curiosity? How do you see it?

S. No not really, the same stuff I took and that's about it. I wouldn't *try anything, you'd get a habit, I just don't trust it. (what about tablets such as jellies and stuff?)... no, I've heard too many bad things about them, that's why I wouldn't touch them.*

I. Do you ever think about stopping though? Or do you think you'll carry on?

S. Oh, carry on, it's because I like taking drugs when I go out, everyone takes drugs when they go out, it just brightens up the night.

I. So if you were told you had to stop could you stop?

S. Yes, definitely.

I. Do you see yourself as addicted at all?

S. No, I've never been addicted to anything else.

I. What does that mean for you?

S. It means I'm drinking nearly every weekend... (why?)... I like getting drunk, I like going into pubs and having a good laugh with your friends and going home drunk.

I. Why is that do you think?

S. You forget about what's happened during the week and that...

I. So how much do you drink?

S. Quite a lot. I drink Budweiser and vodka.

I. So what makes you decide whether your going to drink lager or spirits.

S. I know if I take both Budweiser and Vodka I won't get a hangover the next morning.

I. But how much do you drink?

S. I drink about twelve bottles of Becks/Bud and about eight or nine vodkas a night.

I. So why do you drink to that extent? Do you go out to get pissed or do you find that after a couple you can't stop?

S. It's just once you get to a certain level anyway you just keep drinking anyway, you don't really know too much about what you're doing.

I. Why do you do that do you think?

S. I don't really know, it's just company that's it and a lot of us do drink, so we just do it to be sociable, and we all end up steaming.

I. Do you see it at all as a problem?

S. No, no...

Commentary

The tone of the overall discourse is *hedonistic;* when the interviewee addresses the issue of emotional tone, this centres around fun and enjoyment ("It's just something I like doing. It's fun, it's good fun"). The interviewee makes little attempt to justify use in terms of a reaction to a troubled life history, so the timescale is time present. Although the interviewee reports taking drugs or alcohol sometimes as a response to boredom or a "bad day", this is seen as a deliberate act and *generalisability* is low; drug use is not presented as an inevitable response to a cluster of unfavourable life circumstances. The discourse is *purposive* (intoxication is the desired end) and *volitional* (the acts are carried out "on purpose"). Finally, whilst the interviewee believes people become addicted to certain classes of drugs, his personal use is *non-addicted* and the suggestion that he might be addicted is explicitly denied. The interviewee insists that he could stop if required to do so ("So if you were told or had to stop, could you stop?" "Yes definitely") and that his drug use is non-problematic ("Do you see it at all as a problem?" "No, no...").

Example of type 2 discourse

I. *So how much have you been drinking recently?*

S. *I had a right skinful last night, I've not been too bad, I've been taking it quite easy but I do go off the rails. I just love a drink in the afternoons and after that I need a whole night's sleep to sleep it off.*

I. *Why the afternoons?*

S. *I don't know. I just fancy a pint and I just go for a couple and I'll have three pints and it shuts at 4 so I'll order two pints on last orders – I think if it was open all day I would just have a couple of pints and go away but I'm a clockwatcher, you have to get as much down your neck as possible to beat the bell. I think it's just years of getting into that way of drinking. I found my drinking eased up when the all day drinking came in Scotland because although we all went mad on it at first, we were blootered every day, but after about 6 months you began to realise you could have a drink any time. It's a much more relaxed way of drinking. I am a clock watcher and I try to beat the bell.*

I.   *Presumably there are pubs open in the afternoons?*

S.   *Oh aye, but I prefer clubs for the price and the company.*

I.   *So what problems have you been having with your drinking?*

S.   *I do get depressed on occasions although I've not been as bad lately. If I'm having a drinking spree, not a session a few days, I get very short tempered, not violent but verbally abusive. I've not got time for anything or anybody. I want to shut the world off and go to bed and go to sleep. I don't answer phones, I don't want to make arrangements to do anything.*

I.   *So when you drink is it on your mind that you shouldn't be?*

S.   *It was a pre-arranged do, a masonic affair, and it was with this guy who's just a pig with drink and we really went to town. But it's more the crack than anything else. I wasn't out of control drunk. I did have a good drink but I don't drink to a stupor, I like to keep control. I'm not the sort of person who loses it, I keep myself within control.*

I.   *So what are you hoping to get from coming in here today?*

S.   *I initially wanted, and I still do want, to control my drinking which before I started coming here I wasn't able to do. Rod was telling me about the long-term effect of alcohol, so I imagine we will pick up on that.*

I.   *Are you happy with the way things are going?*

S.   *Aye, I was very annoyed when I was forgotten about. I didn't want to be there in the morning and to get fucked about like that... I was really annoyed, I was thinking what's the point.*

I.   *So what about tablets to come down?*

S.   *I can't get tablets because I've overdosed three times.*

Commentary

The transcript comes from a heavy drinker in the early stages of agency/treatment contact. The type 2 nature of the conversion is identified primarily by the *contradictory* or inconsistent tone of the discourse. This is particularly evident with respect to the issue of *control,* with the respondent suggesting that consumption is both controlled *and* not controlled. ("..I like to keep control.

I'm not the sort of person who loses it, I keep myself within control"; followed in the next sentence by, "I initially wanted, and still do want, to control my drinking which before I started coming here I wasn't able to do..."). *Hedonism* is also mixed. The speaker refers to a number of drink-related problems, including depression, but also suggests there is some pleasure still left in the activity ("I just love to drink in the afternoon"). In terms of *time*, there is some reference to past events, but no long-term or historical attributional explanation of the type that characterises later stages of this model. Finally, there is no consistent (non-contradictory) self-ascription of *addiction.*

Example of type 3 discourse

I. *Can you tell me what it is you've been taking?*

S. *Well, I started at the age of seventeen and I was drinking all my pocket money – whisky and at that time it was heavy beer... the heavy beer was (?)... you were skint, mostly from Sunday to Friday and it started again. I don't know exactly at what age I became an alcoholic, I think it would be maybe about fifteen years ago. I didn't know I was an alcoholic...*

I. *What do you mean by an alcoholic?*

S. *I was taking the shakes and sweats. It was after the break-up of my first marriage which I knew would happen eventually anyway – I wanted (out) of my marriage. I was a long distance truck driver at the time and I wanted to stay (?)... I always had to be finished in time at night to go for my drink, it didn't matter how tired I was, I must have a drink. On a couple of occasions I was so tired – a couple of pints of beer and I wet the bed (went to bed?). I went home so tired and drunk I set a bed on fire. Still didn't realise I was an alcoholic and... after the break-up of my marriage which I wasn't in favour of to begin with, I started drinking very heavily. Sometimes I'd have to drink half a bottle of whisky before I could shave myself. I was taking a drink to work with me – to have when I was finished in case I was going to end up somewhere kind of desolate... (?) pub... I made sure I had something with me.*

I thought it was just to relax. I didn't realise it was a compulsion. That went on for quite a while, quite a while quite a number of years until about five years ago, almost five years ago. I took a fit.. (?) to bed, I knew nothing about it. My wife, my present wife, sent for an ambulance: I'd taken a heart attack and when I came round, the ambulance driver said "I think you've taken a wee seizure and the best thing you can do is send for your panel doctor". So I explained to him what had been happening to me – I'd fallen in a hole – took my cardigan and put it over my head and I was convulsing and the ambulance man said I'd taken a convulsion. I said "No, I tripped over the draught excluder" and he looked at me and said "What draught excluder?"

I was going to my work... I'd left one job on constant day shift, twenty four hours a day on to a night trunk (?)...with a good firm. I was sometimes going to work and the alcohol was still in my system – no' realising it. I felt a bit stupid but I was some-times travelling maybe down the M6 and I was hearing music and I (thought it was??)...my wee radio – I always had a drink with me for when I was finished...

I. *So, I mean, do you still enjoy drinking?*

S. *No. I haven't enjoyed drinking for years.*

I. *So what do you get out of it when you take a drink now?*

S. *Oblivion.*

I. *Is that what you are looking for?*

S. *I don't know, I don't know what I'm looking for.*

I. *Can you make a decision at the time, when you start drinking or is it just you walk past a pub and can't stop yourself?*

S. *Well, this year I've hardly been in a pub. I spent about five weeks sitting in the house. All I was doing was washing and shaving... going off my head. I got to the stage where I couldn't even go out myself and certain other people were asking... they didn't realise... and I was probably (?), I was oblivious to the fact. I wasnae caring, I was saying to them I didn't want to go out – it was just a (sounds like a 'stibble')... and sending people to cash... One morning I went through it myself, just before I started hiding... was taking panic attacks. I got the book cashed and my first dive was for an off-licence and it was only eight o'clock and I couldn't get the book cashed until nine (?) I managed to get into the shop... and there was a church just about fifty yards away and it was only another journey... alone. I went and sat on the church stair and opened a can of beer... anyway I managed to drink the can of beer and put the empty can in my* pocket and take it home with me. My room was littered with empty super lager tins. I managed to put them out every now and again, but I was making up my bed and finding cans of beer were hidden – to have the next morning when I woke up, to try and steady me up, you know – to go for more beer. And then I decided it was time to see my doctor... so that was me. He told me to go home and pack a bag... They brought me up to the Alcohol and Drugs Unit and it was a doctor and a nurse from... came doon – I'd had two cans of beer... to see a doctor – Dutch courage. The doctor was a gentleman. Anyway I got to the ward and it was a doctor from (name of Scottish town). The doctor said to me "Have you had a drink this morning?" I said "Yes!" He said, "Just go back into the ambulance and go home and come back up here tomorrow sober, under your own steam. So I went home and all it did was drive me to another drink. So I had a drink and got up next morning – two of them had to help me to the bus stop and one of them came all the way up – two of my mates. Took me right up to the hospital – they admitted me to (name of hospital) – came back and admitted there had been a mistake, I should have been in (name of another facility). So I was medicated in (hospital name) and transferred to (hospital name) was medicated again and I was medicated all that day. Got up next morning, still... I'd had about thirteen Librium and then they cut it to six and then they cut it down gradually from 10 ml gms to 5. I was fine by the end of the Wednesday – Tuesday last week was the last day of the treatment so Wednesday I was fine and Thursday I started to rattle again. I climbed up on to a table to get a piece of cardboard to keep a window open and I was very badly rattled and I couldn't get back off the top of the table. So they started nursing duty that night, started the medication again and gave me some tablets. That was on the Thursday night... 20 milligrams.. I done well.

On the Friday night I wasnae too bad on the Friday but on Friday night they said well, "I don't think you are just right yet so I'll give you 10 milligrams tonight", so that was the last medication I had. So Saturday and Sunday I was great, you know, they got me in early this morning. I think it was due to maybe it would be one more... in this unit... my stomach was going and I was a wee bit shaky we'll say it's no very clever at all. Anyway, that's about the story of my life.

I.   So, do you see yourself managing to stop?

S.   *Well, I used to be able to stop myself. I could wean myself off. I could stop drinking... now I can't go for a day, two any more. And I was on top of the world, I was a brand new man but it's trying to get it into my brain that I canny take alcohol – I just canny handle it now – it's turning me into a complete wreck. That's just about it...*

I.   *So you are determined this time you are going to stop it.*

S.   *Well, I'm going to try.*

I.   *Good. Right that's fine.*

Commentary

The diagnostic functional features of this discourse come earlier rather than later in the text, the latter part of the transcript being largely taken up with personal narrative. This narrative extends the length of the conversion. It appears that conversations of type 3, and sometimes type 4, are often longer than other types due to the tendency of respondents to embark on lengthy self-disclosure narratives; this fact in itself may help as an identifier at some future stage of the development of the proposed model.

The discourse is identified as type 3 by the following features. Drinking is explained by repeated reference to *time past,* with a causal chain extending back to childhood. There is high *generalisabilty,* with reference to a number of causal factors in the development of the problem, including work problems, loneliness, and an unsatisfactory marriage. There is no reference to enjoyment so *hedonism* is low ("I haven't enjoyed drinking for years") and the behaviour is seen as *non-volitional* ("...I didn't realise it was a compulsion..."). Finally, there is *addicted self-ascription* ("I didn't know I was an alcoholic...").

Example of type 4 discourse

I.   *Can you tell me what you were taking then (name)?*

S.   *I was drinking anything. Lager, cider...*

I.   *So why were you drinking?*

S.   *At the start it was... I was thirteen or fourteen years (old) when*

I started drinking. It was at weekends and it was just for the kick... that was it... just for a kick.

I. *Were you influenced by your friends?*

S. *Me and my mates we were all... we'd get a couple of cans and a bottle of cider and then we started getting more and more, it just carried on then it started getting worse.*

I. *Why did it start to get worse? What do you mean by that?*

S. *Well, I had nae money... what it was... as soon as I got my wages on a Friday and right after work I'd go to the pub, then it would be all day on the Saturday then the Sunday till I had no money left. Sunday afternoon, once that money had ran out I could tap more money and it ended up I would miss my Mondays, I was missing my Mondays the whole time. My boss even says that... he said... you better get something done about yourself, go to AA or something.*

I. *What made you drink like that?*

S. *I don't know it's just... I just enjoyed it. Because I was enjoying it and I was with all my mates...*

I. *So what makes you decide to drink now?*

S. *No... what it was, last year I got assaulted last year and at night time I couldnae get to sleep after the assault and I ended up drinking because I couldnae get to sleep at night. It gave me confidence and it helped me to get to sleep at night. I couldnae go out unless I had a drink in me.*

I. *So why do you decide to seek help? Why did you decide to come to (treatment facility)? Why now?*

S. *I actually... I thought to myself it was best to go back.*

I. *What was the deciding factor?*

S. *I don't know it's just... even my ma says to me, "Look it's too heavy; go and see a doctor or something," and the doctor got me to come here.*

I. *Have you tried to stop in the past?*

S. *Aye, I've tried a couple of times. I've been to one of these groups before but I only lasted three weeks and then I went back on the drink again.*

I. *Why did you do that do you think?*

S. *I don't know what it was. I just wanted a drink and that was it. I just liked to drink because I was sweating and shaking, you know I was shaking I was like that... at the night time I was* sweating in my bed, and I thought I need to go and get a drink. And first thing, as soon as seven o'clock came in the morning I was up getting a carry out.

I   Was that just to square you up?

S.   It was to make me try and get to sleep again. See when I came off the drink which was three to four days I couldnae get to sleep. I was tossing and turning once I'd come off it. I would be lucky if I could get an hour's sleep during the night.

I.   Were you... are you.. taking any drugs or anything?

S.   No, no, no, I'm getting the chlor... something or other off the doctor it's supposed to help you come off the drink. It helps you sleep. But I'm coming off them now.

I.   So how do you see yourself in terms of your drinking?

S.   Well I'm starting to feel that bit better... you know what I mean, better... I used to be borrowing money, now this time I'm lending it out. I have money to give somebody a lend of it.

I.   Do you see yourself as in control of your drinking?

S.   Eh, I don't know. I can walk by a pub and go into a pub. I'd like to be able to take a pint, but it wouldnae be a pint, it would end up going on to more and more.

I.   So what you're saying is that you just need that one and that would start you off again?

S.   ... I was out last night that was it, I just had two pints and that was all I had, and I went up the road. I had more money in my pocket to buy me a drink but I didn't....

I.   So you feel in control that way?

S.   I feel as if I'm starting to get into control.

I.   Was there ever a time in the past when you could take one or two pints and leave it at that without drinking to excess?

S.   No...(?)... in the past. I could have just one, two or three and go up the road.

I.   How do you see it? Do you see it as an illness?

S.   I think it's an illness... you're addicted... it's an addiction ain't it? You feeling bad... (something)... it's more like a medicine.

I.   How do you mean?

S.   If you're feeling bad and then you have a couple of cans you feel brand new again, you're back to yourself.

I.   So are you looking to stop completely or do you want to be a social drinker or what?

S. Well I'd like to be a social drinker, but I think if I become a social drinker I might be able to chuck it altogether... just cut it down... without being unsociable just cut it right down. If you go for a drink once in a blue moon or whatever.

I. Do you think you'll be able to do that then?

S. I don't know. I couldn't tell you.

I. How do you mean?

S. Well I done it last night so; but I couldnae tell ye (as) regards the future.

I. So do you think about the future in terms of being a social drinker? How do you see it?

S. No I don't think about the future. I just take it day to day.

I. Why is that?

S. I don't know what's going to happen in the future... I could walk out today and get hit by a bus or whatever...

I. So in regards to your drinking do you think you might go back to drinking heavily or stop completely?

S. I'm no bothered about my drinking now. But may be once tomorrow comes I'll feel different.

I. Is there anything that might trigger off your drinking heavily?

S. Well, I don't know, it's up to myself. If I want to go for a pint I'll go for a pint... if I don't I won't. I feel as if I can control it like that, that's it. But that's what I'm saying... I don't know if I'll be like that again... know what I mean? Anything could happen to me again, I don't know, or something could happen to my family, and I could turn back again... know what I mean.

I. But at the moment though you feel quite in control?

S. Aye... I feel in control aye.

Commentary

The most striking features of this discourse, which identify it as a type 4 are the *contradictoriness* voiced by the interviewee over a number of issues, particularly control, and the affirmation of the *addiction* label which differentiates it from a type 2. ("I think it's an illness... you're addicted... it's an addiction ain't it... you feeling bad... it's more like a medicine".) The major phenomenological characteristic of the discourse is of someone being pulled in two opposing directions, and there are numerous examples of this. The drinking is both *purposive* and *non-purposive;* the desired outcome is abstinence *and* social drinking; alcohol is the cause of problems but also a desired source of pleasure. Finally, the drinking is both controllable, but likely to become uncontrollable at any moment ("Anything could happen to me again, I don't know, or something could happen to my family, and I could turn back again... know what I mean?" {function: so *naturally* that would start me off again, know what I mean?} "But at the moment though you feel quite in control?" "Aye, I feel in control.") Perhaps the most disturbing aspect of this transcript, however, is the clear battle between an abstinence discourse, and a return-to-controlled-drinking discourse ("I'd like to be able to take a pint, but it would nae be a pint... it would end up going on to more and more..." and "... I'd like to be a social drinker but I think if I become a social drinker I might be able to chuck it altogether..." "Do you think you'll be able to do that then?" "I don't know. I couldn't tell you..."). The potential for relapse in this cell is clearly demonstrated.

Example of type 5 positive discourse

I. *So what is it you are taking now?*

S. *Absolutely nothing.*

I. *No?*

S. *No... I've finished the methadone script that I was on six or seven weeks ago. I thought it would be more but I don't take any medication now at all.*

I. *So how did you find it?*

S. *Well it wasn't as difficult as I thought it was going to be. I thought especially the physical side. Basically I just really wanted to do it, and because of that will it was a lot easier than I thought it was going to be. The physical side does drain you a bit, you know, you do get tired and feeling achey and all the rest of it but, you know, if you want to do it you'll put up with it for a week or whatever. It's a week or so you know. From since then it's been really good, I don't think there's been a day when I've said, you know, "I really can't handle this" or anything like that, you know, but there again I had my music and things to get into which filled a big gap which has really helped to take my mind off everything else and I think that's the main thing. If you've got something else to do to fill in your time then I don't think you have any problem and also, obviously, if you really want to do it, you know... but I found it... I didn't think it was going to be as easy as it was.*

I. *So why did you decide you wanted to do it?*

S. *Well because I have a young daughter and I didn't enjoy feeling the way I did, feeling physically ill all the time. Money, family also, they knew that I was taking heroin and it was either my family or heroin, you know. Basically I just really began to hate the stuff, really hate it because of what it was...*

I. *While you were still on it?*

S. *Yeah. Yeah, it doesn't... it's not enjoyment after a while... it's a need and to have to rely on something like that and to have to have it every day... it just takes it all out of you, you know. You're waking up thinking "where am I going to get the money today?" and stuff like that, you know. It's really just no way to live, you know, to have to be thinking about things like that all the time and that's all you ever think about, you know. I found that really tiring especially with having a daughter and all the rest of it. It was like no time for anything else unless you got your hit sorted, and, I don't know maybe I had more of a con-science than the people I was associating with. I just couldn't do it any more and I had to get out.*

I. *When did you stop enjoying it?*

S. *I think it was pretty early on I became an addict, yeah at least two or three months after I had started taking it regularly... and one particular day I sort of woke up and didn't have any money or any heroin or anything and it was then that I really started hating (it)... what it made you feel and things, you know.*

I. *Were you still actually enjoying the effects of it?*

S. *You do it because you have to, because if you don't you feel physically ill; and you DON'T do it because you're going to get off, you're going to get high... no... you do it because you have to, to make you feel alright and you don't get high any more you... just feel alright, you know. But yeah if you took extra amounts you'd probably get high but that's more money and that's just more to come off, you know, so you do stop enjoying it and for me I stopped enjoying it quite soon after I started using it purely because people are always looking for (something)... I've heard people say that they's always looking for that first high and it never comes back, you know, you become physically dependent on it so you have to have it and that's what takes the enjoyment away. Yeah, it was pretty soon after I became, you know, addicted that it wasn't like a pleasure anymore, you know. It wasn't a pleasure at all.*

I. *So how long have you been off drugs for?*

S. *About a year, all in all.*

I. *What made you decide that was how you wanted to do it?*

S. *Because it was available and it means that I didn't have to spend any money, mostly.*

I. *Was there any point when you were going for methadone, that you were using it as a way of increasing your choices?*

S. *No it wasn't... I didn't use the methadone just to keep me going, if you like, I chose to ask for a methadone script because it meant that I could get myself out of a rut, financially,... not have to feel guilty about, you know, spending money on things and for me to have a methadone script when I've got one (?) is... it was a really excellent help. It took a lot of weight off my shoulders, you know, and I think there is... I mean I started off on 50 ml a day and I honestly thought that was too much 'cause I thought "that's a lot to come off", ... you know they have to reduce the things but (name) explained that she, you know, she was looking at a year, even a lot longer, so after I got used to the idea then it was okay but I didn't like taking as much as that every day.*

I. *How did you feel?*

S. *Just normal. You just didn't feel ill. When I first started taking it, you know, every day I did get high 'cause obviously it's, you know, pure stuff. You know, you get used to it, you know how it's going to make you feel so you just sort of get on with it, but yeah... unless you take a really large amount it just made you feel normal, you didn't feel ill or you wouldn't be sweating or anything like that. You were able to do most things without worrying about anything.*

I. *Was it always just heroin you took?*

S. *Yeah... Well, I'm saying yeah. You know I experimented with speed and smoked hash but heroin was the main one.*

I. *Do you think you could ever use drugs recreationally again?*

S. *Yeah. I smoke hash quite often. I like to have a drink of alcohol, but I mean this is the bit I can't understand... and other people, well I mean I know a couple who've actually come off... but they can't smoke a joint or they can't have a drink or they can't have a line of speed or something like that because they honestly believe it's going to take them back, you know.*

I. *Do you think the agency's doctrined (?) people to think like that?*

S. *Yeah... yeah I do actually. I think, you know you get it drummed into you that you come off and that's it, that is it. It's all to do with self, with inner-strength, you know, if you... I mean there's no reason, I can't see any reason... I mean if I smoke a joint I don't immediately think "God I want a hit of heroin", you know, I don't and it's the same with the drink or whatever I think... it's just... I think it's personally, I think it's a weakness... if somebody says "Well I can't have drink or smoke or whatever because it'll get me back to the heroin" because I don't believe that. That's just not believing in yourself enough, you know. I mean I can have a smoke and I can have a drink and I'm really, really quite happy because I didn't want to be a heroin addict anyway... so taking a step back and knowing what I've stepped back from, a joint and a smoke is perfectly acceptable. So that's something I just don't understand about... I mean if they are strong enough to come off heroin in the first place, you know, then they must have some kind of will, you know, so that's an attitude I don't understand. But everybody's different I suppose.*

I. *Will you ever try heroin again?*

S. *I don't think I will because I couldn't have got much higher than I've already been. I think if the opportunity ever arose I would probably think about it but I'd probably, you know, would then step back and say "well... because I know how it gets a hold of you"... and it does... it creeps up on you and you don't realise, you know, but it's like a big shadow, you know, it just comes swooping over and...*

I. *How do you feel now about experimenting with drugs, say crack, ecstasy or whatever, you know, that anything can be tried?*

S. *Well I haven't tried ecstasy and I've never tried crack before and to be quite honest those two drugs really frighten me, especially the crack because I mean heroin... you go a totally different way, you know, you slow down but with crack you... you know people tell me that your heart rate goes up to a ridiculous rate. No, they frighten me because it could just be like one time, you know I mean but ecstasy I know people who've taken it and I mean that's a dance drug anyway. People say it's pointless trying to* take it and just sitting in the house or whatever, you know, you've got to be out at a party or a rave or something... but I mean I'm not into... I mean I've taken acid before and things like that but "E" and the (something) that are full of crack and you become allergic, you can have an allergic reaction and things like that, you know. No I don't think I'll ever try crack or "E". I don't feel I have to, I need to, you know.

I. *Do you still think of yourself as an addict?*

S. No. No, not now. I know that I have been a heroin addict but, when I decided I wanted to come off I felt like an addict then... but as soon as I started you know reducing the methadone and things like that. When I hadn't had methadone for a whole week and I was completely straight and clean you just go "Well I'm not an addict any more, I've done it". So, yeah you say, yeah I was but, you know, but I don't think... I mean that's it, a girl I was talking to just a couple of weeks ago, she said "I am ill and I will always..." Yeah she was saying that she has got this illness for the rest of her life and it's like she can't have a joint or whatever because she thinks that'll be it, she'll be straight back into the heroin but she obviously feels that she will always be a heroin addict. I don't feel like that, you know. I'm not a heroin addict because I don't take heroin, you know, I don't have any more... so that's the difference, you know. But I mean a lot of people have come off and they will always have the attitude of "well it's an illness and I will always be a heroin addict". I don't believe that, you know.

I. *Do you think places like (name of agency) make it worse? The way they define people as addicts?*

S. I think what, to me, what's happened is instead of saying your addiction is selfish and its self-abuse they've said your addiction is an illness and I think people have used the illness thing to, you know, be easier on themselves and say "I'm ill" instead of "It's my own fault", you know. But maybe, you know, that works with people but really because it's such a taboo subject anyway I think you've really got to be straight and hard with people and say "well yeah it is your own stupid fault", you know, 'cause it is. Nobody says you have to stick a needle in your arm or you have to take this, you know. It's your own choice. So if it works, if people come off thinking that it was an illness then fine... but I mean we all know really it's not an illness... it's a self-induced thing, that only you can get out of, you know. I mean... yeah...

you can get help and counselling and all the rest of it but it's you at the end of the day who has to say, right, you know, I'm going to do it.

Commentary

This type five positive discourse is identified by the fact that whilst the speaker self-attributes *addiction,* this is seen as something in the past. ("I think it was pretty early on I became an addict..."; followed later by, "Do you still think of yourself as an addict?" "No, no, not now. I know that I have been a heroin addict... When I hadn't had methadone for a whole week... you just go, `Well, I'm not an addict anymore, I've done it.'"). There is some return of *hedonism,* as indicated by the fact that the speaker reports being able to use alcohol and certain other drugs for pleasure, with no long term implications ("Yeah. I smoke hash quite often. I like to have a drink..."; and "... I can have a smoke and I can have a drink and I'm really quite happy..."). Whilst the speaker refers to the *need* to use drugs at various points in her career, and to physical dependence, there is a strong vein of choice and *purposiveness* throughout. This aspect is the strongest point of the discourse and there are numerous examples throughout the text. The sense of personal agency is particularly strong. ("... it's you at the end of the day who has to say right, you know, I'm going to do it..."). Finally, the speaker also shows a grasp, albeit a somewhat unsympathetic grasp, of functional attribution, as revealed in the last paragraph. ("... I think people have used the illness thing to, you know, be easier on themselves..." and "... if people come off, thinking it was an illness, then fine but I mean we all know really it's an illness, it's a self-induced thing...") The functionality and consequences of the type 3 discourse are clearly understood by this interviewee.

Example of type 5 negative discourse

It has been mentioned at a number of points that we obtained no clear or usable examples of our hypothesised type 5 negative discourse, although its existence is clearly inferred. However, the work of Crugeira in Portugal has been referred to at a number of points. Crugeira is undertaking work with people living in shanty-town settlements in and around Lisbon and has come up with a fatalistic type of discourse in some numbers, quite unlike anything we obtained in the U.K. The discourse appears to be volitional, hedonistic to a degree, but fatalistic in the sense that no other future is envisaged beyond continued drug use and ultimately death. Crugeira believes this may be the elusive type 5 negative.

In searching through the more difficult-to-code transcripts, the following was identified by the author as being somewhat odd. Crugeira subsequently identified it as a type 5 negative, and certainly as having certain points in common with some of the Portuguese transcripts.

I. *So how do you find that? How's it going?*

S. *It disnae. It gets my by when I'm naughty and that but it's no a' (all) I use.*

I. *What else are you using apart from that?*

S. *Coke and speed... coke with speed... it's all the time.*

I. *How does your methadone affect that?*

S. *If ah didnae have my methadone I'd need double the amount of everything I use.*

I. *How much... (pause)... do you use?*

S. *Only once a week... hash every... since I was about 12.*

I. *Yes, but I mean, like you know, on a day to day basis what makes you go out and buy stuff?*

S. *Actually, I've (?) had the meth to be quite honest... high at it(?)... although you've no got the urgency to go out and rob someone... there's no high and I'm always looking for a high.*

I. *And why do you bother with the methadone?*

S. *Because as I said, if I didn't have that to get me to a certain level I'd struggle to get out of my bed and it makes you commit twice as much crime... know what I mean...*

I. *You need the meth?*

S. *It's a saviour to me.*

I. *Why don't you keep...?*

S. *(interrupts)... see when I get the meth, the first I got, see I sat down and cheered up... aw fuck, Mary Mother of Joseph...*

I. *Why do you think you are taking drugs anyway – for the high (hype)?*

S. *I think, I know I'm hiding from something – I don't know what – I'll need to remember what crime...*

I. *Why do you do it now?*

S. *It's amazing – I'm trying to remember...*

I. *Why do you think you go in... (unclear)... drugs? Why do you take speed and cannabis?*

S. *Fun. All the different kinds of stones... why not... why I drink... why I keep women.*

I. *Are you looking for... to stop?*

S. *That's my hobby... people.*

I. *So don't you see it as a problem. Are you quite happy with that?*

S. *There's a problem if I can't get it...*

I. *There's a problem if you can't get enough and you had to enrol, or because...*

S. *It's just that without the meth... and I was injecting with smack and that, I had to get up in the morning, feeling rough and wondering where the next one was coming from. With the meth you can lie in and you know it's there for to get up to. And that'll help you alright... if you think that you don't need to bother, you can just stay in bed.*

I. *Are you strict with your methadone, do you take it exactly the 90 ml every day?*

S. *Never. Never take it like that.*

I. *So what do you do, do you take it all on the first day?*

S. *No, no. I take it different all the time. I dinna stick to a routine. That way you get nothing off it.*

I. *Too tough.*

S. *Uhu. That's what I'm saying. I wouldnae stick to a regular thing where you get nothing off it.*

I. *Do you ever buy methadone?*

S. *Ay. I dae. If I get a bargain like a sealed bottle.*

I. *You can get a stone from methadone if you take enough of it. How much do you have to take to get that? To get a stone off it.*

S. *It depends on what way you have been taking it – me I never stick to the same way – I'm on a 90 ml a day now and, may be for three days just taking it for (something) I've got something else. Then when I've nae money I'll take the 90 ml.*

I. *What have you taken today?*

S. *Speed, this morning.*

I. When you go to buy it, what makes you decide what you are going to buy?

S. If I have a separate team with me (?) I'm glad of what I can get and as the day goes on it usually works out OK.

I. So do you feel quite in control?

S. I'm always in control.

I. Do you want to stop?

S. Naw, I couldnae. I'm hiding from something and I don't know what it is.

I. Do you ever think about the future?

S. Ay, about what I was going (to do?) the night (tonight).

I. (pause)

S. Well, I do when I think about my kids, I've got 12 kids. Doing the best I can, being understanding, in the time I've got left.

Commentary

Since no clear profile as yet exists for this discourse, the comments that can be made are limited. The profile is clearly not as hypothesised. The discourse appears to be both *hedonistic* (the basic motive appears to be to get "high") and *purposive*; the interviewee says, "I am always in control". He also says that he does not want to stop, and that he is "hiding from something". The drug use therefore appears to serve some ill-defined but fatalistic function. There is no explicit reference to *addiction* and the interviewee plans the future with regard to the limited life-span he sees as remaining. Whether the above will prove to have the salient features of type 5 negative remains to be seen.

8

Predicting
Behaviour
From Speech

The usefulness of any model of the type proposed hangs crucially on its ability to predict behaviour. The reader does not require a reminder that finding links between what people say and what they do is a notoriously difficult task; virtually any basic social psychology text includes a discussion of the relative failure of attitudes to predict behaviour. The fact that among senior members of health boards, politicians, and other important groups, attitude change is still frequently viewed as the primary key to behaviour change illustrates more the power of this act of faith, than its power as illustrated in empirical studies. The solution to this difficulty is often seen as residing in more sophisticated models which re-examine the attitude-behaviour link in greater detail. It seems likely, for example, that the notion of attitude (assuming one accepts attitude as a defensible notion) is itself multi-faceted, and also that a number of important intervening variables mediate the relationship between a measured attitude and an observed behaviour. The Health Beliefs Model and the theories of Reasoned Action and of Planned Behaviour, are classic examples of attempts to find a solution via this route. Such solutions usually involve the postulation of a number of intervening variables inhabiting the space between expressed attitude and behaviour, which are believed to mediate the nature and degree of any relationship between the verbal (attitude) and behavioural spheres.

It appears however that to many practitioners in the field prediction in the above sense requires exploration of the specific question "Did this person in fact do what they said or implied they would do?" (i.e. exploration of the semantic relationship between statements and behaviour) rather than the more general question "Is there a relationship between what this person said and what they subsequently did?" (i.e. exploration of the statistical relationship between statements and behaviour). These two questions are not the same. In the first instance, a relationship would be inferred, or not inferred, on the basis of data which are coded in terms of the semantics of utterances; whereas in the second case such inference would be made on a statistical basis alone regardless of semantic considerations. In a classical sense, it is the latter approach which is psychometrically the most defensible. Anastasi, in her classic text of 1961 for example, writes, "It should be noted in this connection that the test items need not resemble closely the behaviour the test is to predict. It is only necessary that an empirical correspondence be demonstrated between the two".

For example, from the point of view which takes semantics as being primary (i.e. an experimenter's assertions about what a statement "really means"), the finding that subjects who agreed with an item such as "I think that going to the doctor is a good idea" in fact never went to the doctor, would be interpreted in isolation as a prima facie failure of attitude to predict behaviour. In fact, statistically, no such inference could be made in the absence of data from people who actually do go the doctor. In the unlikely event that these latter actually tended to disagree with the statement, then prediction would actually be very high in statistical terms (i.e. going to the doctor would be predicted, statistically, from statements suggesting that this was not a good idea). In other words, semantic prediction and statistical prediction are not the same thing at all. It may well be the case that assumptions based on semantics, rather than on statistics, are often in error since (as we have argued in previous chapters) the experimenter may not understand the contextual constraints surrounding the issue, and thus have no basis for deciding what the response "actually means". Thus, a person who knows nothing about prisons or prisoners might interpret the finding, that people who endorse the statement "Prisons are a good thing" are virtually absent from the prison environment, as a failure of attitude to predict behaviour. In fact if, as may well be the case, people who endorse such a statement come exclusively and commonly from outside the prison environment, statistical prediction might be quite high. Thus, outside or independent knowledge is necessary to interpret these two fictitious scenarios, and whether the expressed attitude predicts the behaviour or not cannot be inferred from the words alone, which in the two examples given are semantically in opposition. That is, people who think that doctors are a good idea tend to go to the doctors; whilst people who think that prison is a good idea tend NOT to go to prison.

The above examples border on the ridiculous since all of us have some general awareness and independent understanding of doctors, and of the prison system. Nonetheless it makes sense in the interests of science to harbour as few preconceptions as possible, especially in an area where drug problems are routinely researched by people who do not have such problems, and possibly no personal experience of the phenomenon in question nor of the contexts in which it takes place. (N.B. this is not the argument that only drug users can do useful drug research; merely that researchers should be aware that some of the assumptions they make may be different from, or even opposite to, the assumptions made by the objects of their studies, and that it is possible to be unaware of that fact.) The present chapter, therefore, reverts to Anastasi's classic approach in seeking statistical links between what people say and what they do, without any recourse to whether such a link is manifested in the surface semantics of what is said. Face validity, therefore, is seen here as the weakest of bases for hypothesis validation, a standpoint which is compatible with the philosophy of discourse explained in earlier chapters. Furthermore, an approach which suspends any need for the inference of "truth" or "real meanings" is not a radical suggestion. Far from being an anarchistic and iconoclastic blast of post-modernism, it has its roots in classic psychological and psychometric theory. Consequently, whether a statement such as "I cannot stand heights"; or even "I like fried eggs" predicts hang-gliding is seen as a matter for statistical, rather than semantic, analysis. And notwithstanding any semantic arguments to the contrary, either statement could in principle be an excellent predictor.

In light of the above, the present chapter now explores the possibility of using the functional discursive model described in the previous section as a tool in the clinical or counselling setting. The model argues that "drugspeak" may be conceptualised as a series of types of conversations, the veridical status of which is unknown and unknowable. The data suggest that the system is reliable and replicable in the sense that such conversational types can be recognised with some consistency by people trained in the use of the method; also that such agreement extends to the dimensions underlying the system, so that such agreement is more than skin deep. The practical usefulness of the system however derives from the extent to which empirical relationships can be found between types of discourse and other things of interest for the study of drug problems. The remainder of this chapter gives an account of some preliminary attempts to address this issue, to assess in general terms the likely usefulness of the functional discursive approach, and to argue for the importance of further studies to examine the predictive utility of functional discursive modelling in a variety of different contexts.

Extent of drug use

In the present study, no structured method was used to explore and assess quantity/frequency data of the type that characterises most studies. At the start of each interview, subjects were merely asked *"What are you using at the moment?"* and the conversation took its own route from there. Solely on the basis of the transcripts of the taped conversations, raters simply recorded on their coding sheets any drug that was mentioned (a list of drugs was provided on each coding sheet – see Fig. 3). Separate data were collected for subjects closely involved with agencies at the time of interview (the clinical group) and for subjects minimally involved with agencies (the non-clinical group). The distinction between clinical and non-clinical groups is not clear cut, since most long-term users have some agency contact at some time.

On the basis of the transcripts of the conversations, raters placed each drug mentioned on a simple three-point frequency scale (frequent, occasional, none) according to their understanding of what was being said. No specific attempt was made to persuade subjects to "rate" their drug use on a standard scale, the judges ratings being made simply on the basis of a commonsense understanding of the salience attached to different drugs by the speaker in each transcript. In order to discover what drugs were reported as being most commonly used amongst our subjects, we then simply computed the percentage of the sample reporting current use of that drug on a frequent or occasional basis.

The data are of interest not as sources of "facts" as collected by carefully sampled questionnaire studies, but as examples of what might be obtained from a different methodological standpoint. What drugs did our sample tell us they used frequently? To what extent do largely unstructured conversations with an opportunity sample of drug users reflect broader wisdoms? The data shown in Table 4 below indicate that, despite the lack of a consistent or structured method of elicitation, results are obtained that are reliable and that mirror findings collected by more structured methods. Specifically, the data in the table show the relative prevalence of use in the present study by the combined sample of in-agency contact (clinical) and out of agency contact (non-clinical) groups in Glasgow; the data referring to *non-prescribed (street) drugs only*. Also included in the table for comparison purposes are data from the 1994 multi-city study of drug misuse carried out for the Council of Europe by Frischer (Frischer, 1994), one of the foremost epidemiologists in Scotland. Frischer's data are again specific to Glasgow. Frischer's data are interesting from a comparative point of view since his subject pool comprised a mixture of in-agency-contact and out-of-agency contact users roughly in a proportion of two-to-one in favour of agency contacts (see footnote to Table CT20-2-2, page 58). This is roughly comparable to the structure of our own obtained Glasgow sample (N=80 after removal of "alcohol" clients) in which there were 29 (36.3%) non-agency contacts and 51 (63.7%) in agency contact. It should be noted that our own study included people with alcohol problems. These (17.4%) were removed from the data before compiling the present table.

Table 4.

	A	B
Cocaine	17 (7)	0.4. (7)
Ecstasy	26.1 (6)	10.4 (5)
Heroin	89.5 (1)	25.5 (2)
Methadone	35.2 (5)	7.2 (6)
Amphet.	36.1 (4)	14.7 (4)
Temazepam	76.6 (2)	31.6 (1)
Temgesic	44.6 (3)	17.2 (3)

Prevalence of street drug use reported by Frischer (1994) in a Glasgow sample, column A; and prevalence of drug use as coded by judges from transcripts of a sample of Glasgow drug users (column B). Figures indicate proportions of total samples; figures in brackets represent rank-orders.

These data raise a number of interesting issues. Firstly correlations between the two data sets are extremely high. Spearman correlation based on ranks alone yields a rho of 0.93, with a significance for p of 0.003; and, setting aside considerations of data distributions for the time being, Pearson Product-Moment based on the raw data yields r = 0.91 (p = 0.004). Furthermore, the data from Frischer were published in 1994, and our own data collection took place from mid 1993 to late 1994, so there was actual overlap in the data collection exercises; they ought to produce a similar picture. What is more problematic is the differences between the two studies in terms of the actual proportions reported, despite the striking stability in terms of rank-order prevalence.

The most obvious explanations for the differences in the actual numbers obtained are in terms of the methods employed and particularly the time period researched.* However, the most likely explanation for much of the difference would be in terms of the Social Criterion theory outlined in chapter 4. The argument from chapter 4 suggests strongly that data ought to vary as a consequence of subject's social criterion and experimenter's signal strength. Consequently, we would expect differences of the type found to result from differences between the two studies in terms of criterion and signal strength. A forced-choice highly cued method of the type adopted by Frischer would, according to the theory, produce more hits (fewer misses) and more false positives (higher levels of use reported both correctly and incorrectly), whilst a minimally cued and minimally structured method of the type described in this book would produce fewer hits (more misses) and fewer false positives (lower levels of use, and lower incidence of incorrect reports of drug use). Such a theory would be supported by data sets similar to the ones compared above. Indeed, the data show a striking similarity to data sets obtained

---

*It should be noted that in our own study, the opening and only standard question concerned current drug use whereas Frischer asked specific questions about drug use during the last year, thus presenting a larger window. This doubtless accounts for some of the difference between the data sets, although its major impact would be on total drugs used rather than on number of users. Furthermore, in Frischer's study no distinction was made between prescribed and non-prescribed drugs, so it is difficult to be certain about the impact of prescription drugs on those figures. In our own study, respondents usually provided information that made such a distinction possible. This mainly affects the methadone figures. In our own study, inclusion of prescribed methadone raises the sample prevalence figure from 7.2% to 60.6%. Since the methadone data are thus open to some uncertainty, we replicated the above correlations, removing methadone from the list. This yielded correlations of 0.94 (Pearson) and 0.94 (Spearman), p equal to or less than 0.006 in both cases.

from S.D. studies of perceptual processes obtained under differ-ent criterion positions (e.g. McNicol *op. cit.* shows data from a perceptual study characterised by differences in absolute detec-tion rates and perfect between-series correlations p. 21)

The Glasgow data were dealt with in some detail above, since Frischer's data present an excellent opportunity for comparison, despite the problems with arriving at strong conclusions. However, similar regional breakdowns were obtained for Edinburgh, Newcastle, and South Ayrshire. In the absence of comparable contemporary studies of the Frischer type in those areas, similar comparisons are not possible. Nonetheless, given the ordinal reliability of the previous data set, the regional data suggest there may be important regional differences in the salience of different street (non-prescribed) drugs. Amongst the clinical group (those in agency contact for drug problems) the Edinburgh sample gave great prominence to temazepam and diazepam, rather like the Glasgow sample, but little heroin use was reported. In contrast, the Newcastle upon Tyne group gave greatest prominence to temazepam, heroin and amphetamine; and the South Ayrshire group made most frequent mention of temazepam, (street) methadone and amphetamine. It is worth nothing that cannabis use was common amongst all groups, but that alcohol use was most prominent amongst respondents in Glasgow and Newcastle, and least in Edinburgh.

Examination of the regional data show something rather more important than simple prevalence differences. We compared the results obtained for the four locations of the study (Glasgow, Newcastle, Edinburgh and South Ayrshire) in terms of the reported street (non-prescribed) drug use of the clinical and non-clinical samples. Once again using the rank ordering of drugs used as reported by our subjects, we computed correlations between data sets. Table 5 below shows the correlations between the localities for the clinical and non-clinical groups separately.

Table 5. *Correlations (Spearman) between reports of street (non-prescribed) drug use in the four localities; non-clinical and clini-cal groups separately.*

Non-clinical (minimal agency contact)

	Glasgow	Ayr	Edinburgh
Ayr	0.099 (p = .79)		
Edinburgh	0.15 (p = .69)	0.12 (p = .74)	
Newcastle	0.298 (p = .40)	0.57 (p = .08)	0.11 (p = .77)

Table 5 (continued)

Clinical (agency contact)

	Glasgow	Ayr	Edinburgh
Ayr	0.65 (p = .04)		
Edinburgh	0.68 (p = .03)	0.71 (p = .02)	
Newcastle	0.51 (p = .13)	0.83 (p = .003)	0.60 (p = .07)

There is a contrast between the two matrices, with that for the non-clinical group showing 5 out of 6 small and non-significant correlations; that for the clinical group showing 5 out of 6 substantively important and 4 statistically significant correlations. Examination of the raw data shows how this might come about. Firstly, the discourse of those in treatment/agency contact (the clinical group) gives salience to street use of temazepam/diazepam, methadone, and heroin in all regions. By contrast, the "fun drugs" (LSD, ecstasy, cocaine) are seldom referred to in their conversations. This is of particular significance when considering the five-stage discursive model since as will be shown later this pattern of drug use is associated with type-three ("helpless addict") discourse. By contrast, street-drug use by the non-clinical group tends to be more variable in nature, with substantial proportions of the sample in each area making reference to use of ecstasy, amphetamine, and LSD in addition to heroin, methadone and minor tranquilisers. The above data suggest therefore an interaction between drug use and treatment, with treatment being associated with the increased salience of the "treatment" drugs (methadone and tranquillisers) plus heroin. On the basis of our transcriptions, therefore, it is interesting to speculate whether this increased salience derives from a narrowing of the street-drug repertoire, a sort of shortening of the drug shopping list, and an increasing focus at the street level on the maintenance/prescription drugs which agencies tend to provide, plus heroin. If so, a key question here is the extent to which "addicts" present with such a shopping list prior to treatment, or whether treatment itself actually plays a causal role in establishing a pattern of use from which hedonistic or recreational drug use becomes gradually expunged. The pattern of discourse associated with this type of drug use, and especially methadone, is best described by stage three within our proposed model; this type of discourse being characterised by stability, lack of purposiveness and lack of hedonism. By contrast, stage one and stage two conversations tend to be more hedonistic and stage two also more unstable/

contradictory. A possible conclusion from the juxtaposition of pattern of use and mode of explanation, in the light of the above data, is that prescription of opiate substitutes (whilst reducing harm by offering stability, pharmaceutical safety, reduced crime, etc.: see for example Ward, Mattick & Hall, 1992) might sometimes reinforce a stable and hopeless pattern of drug use amongst some users.*

In concluding this first data section, it remains only to reiterate that the method adopted, involving minimally cued conversations with users and their transcription, can produce reliable and systematic data which reflect findings from studies conducted according to a more structured methodology.

The five-stage functional discursive model: empirical support

It will be recalled that judges coded the transcripts in terms of a number of dimensions on their score sheets, the dimensions being (i) attribution of addiction (ii) hedonism (iii) contradictoriness (iv) time (v) physiological reductionism (vi) psychological reductionism (vii) social reductionism (viii) generalisability (ix) purposiveness. Data were also collected from subjects on three occasions, as far as this proved possible. In order to estimate the degree of stability with which the dimensions predicted the stages, and also to look for consistency in terms of those variables showing the greatest predictive power at three different times, three separate multiple regression analyses were carried out, one for each round of data collection.

Since the five-stage model is not underlaid by any dimension which might reasonably be called scalar or even ordinal in nature, an overall analysis would be invalid. However, the model may be conceptualised as falling into two main stages, a "getting worse" stage (stages 1 to 3) and a "getting better" stage (stages

---

*It is interesting to speculate about the possible consequences of prescribing other drugs associated with a more dynamic and purposive pattern of discourse. A more hedonistic pattern of drug use might sometimes actually be advantageous since it is associated with greater purposiveness; or even therapeutically beneficial in the absence of any intention to quit, in the sense that a more mixed drug diet including "fun" drugs might encourage a dynamic and proactive approach to drug use which might have better therapeutic implications.

3 to 5+). Whilst these two broad sections of the model are not exclusive (stage three occurs in both), there is a reasonable assumption of ordinality underlying each half of the model. Noting that the results would not be totally independent by virtue of the inclusion of category 3 in each model, we performed multiple regression analyses on the two halves of the model separately, as a partial solution to the problem of non-linearity in the model as a whole. The results are provided in Table 6 below.*

Table 6 (a)

Results of multiple regression analyses on stages 1–3 of the model, carried out on three separate occasions.

Time 1. Multiple r = 0.95 (p less than 0.0001)

Time 2. Multiple r = 0.98 (p less than 0.0001)

Time 3. Multiple r = 0.98 (p less than 0.0001)

Variables involved:	Time 1.	Addiction, Contradictoriness, Generalisability, Hedonism, Time.
	Time 2.	Addiction, Physiological Reductionism, Hedonism, Generalisability, Contradictoriness.
	Time 3.	Contradictoriness, Generalisability, Physiological Reductionism, Time

Table 6 (b)

Results of multiple regression analyses on stages 3–5 of the model, carried out on three separate occasions.

Time 1. Multiple r = 0.86 (p less than 0.0001)

Time 2. Multiple r = 0.90 (p less than 0.0001)

Time 3. Multiple r = 0.85 (p less than 0.0001)

Variables involved:	Time 1.	Addiction, Contradictoriness, Hedonism, Purposiveness, Time.
	Time 2.	Addiction, Purposiveness, Hedonism, Generalisability, Contradictoriness.
	Time 3.	Addiction, Contradictoriness, Generalisability, Hedonism, Purposiveness.

N.B. All variables in the above tables are listed in descending order of beta-weights.

---

*The reader will recall that five negative discourse (5-) was not obtained in any usable form and so may be ignored for the purpose of this analysis.

The data in Table 6 above show high levels of prediction of stage from clusters of variables; in some cases, extremely high. In fact, what the data show is simply that certain variables are sufficient to define totally certain stages of the model. Thus, within the two halves of the model, contradictoriness defines stage two in the first half of the model, and stage four in the second half. Similarly, addiction reaches a peak in both sets of analyses in stage three. In a sense, therefore, the analysis merely confirms the theoretical model described in the previous chapter. It shows that the judges did in fact use the theoretical model in the way intended, and they did so reliably. The high levels of prediction merely confirm this.

What is of more importance is the fact that certain variables appear consistently in the regression equations whilst others do not. The division of reductionism into three categories clearly adds little to the predictive capability of the model. Physiological reductionism occurs in two of the analyses for the first stage of the model, where it defines the shift from stage two to stage three. It adds nothing to prediction within the second stage of the model. The other species of reductionism (psychological, social) add nothing important to the pattern of prediction at any point, and may thus usefully be discarded in any future research.

On the other hand, the other dimensions occur with some regularity and clearly form the basis on which stage assignments are made. Purposiveness is interesting insofar as it appears as an important predictor throughout the second half of the model (the "getting better" stages), but does not appear to discriminate within the first half of the model; a result which was not anticipated. Addiction, hedonism, generalisability and contradictoriness appear to be key predictors across the entire model.

Discriminant function analyses were also performed for each of the three data collection rounds, on the first and the second halves (as above) of the model, to assess the extent to which the multiple regression equations could correctly assign subjects to stages on the basis of the dimensional data only. For the first half of the model (stages 1 - 3) 95.6% (n = 180), 98% (n = 106) and 97.4% (n = 39) were correctly assigned; and for the second half of the model (stages 3 - 5+) 89.3% (n = 215), 94.6% (n = 166) and 86.1% (n = 65) were correctly assigned respectively.

Differences between the clinical and non-clinical groups

Data were collected on two groups of drug users, which we termed the clinical group and the non-clinical group. The clinical group comprised people who were in agency contact or who came into agency contact during the study. Table 7 below cross-tabulates the clinical and non-clinical groups by the type of discourse they provided, at each of the three interviews.

Table 7

Cross tabulation of group x discourse type, at each of three interviews. (raw frequencies)

Time 1

Stage	1	2	3	4	5+	
Clinical group.	3	12	117	85	6	n=223
Non-clinical group.	27	18	3	4	0	n=52

(chi-square, p less than .0001 for 4 df)

Time 2.

Stage	1	2	3	4	5+	
Clinical group.	2	3	74	79	8	n=166
Non-clinical group.	17	9	1	4	0	n=31

(chi square, p less than .0001 for 4 df)

Time 3.

Stage	1	2	3	4	5+	
Clinical group	3	1	26	33	2	n=65
Non-clinical group	5	3	1	2	1	n=12

(chi square, p less than .0001 for 4 df)

It will be noted in the above table that a highly significant chi-square value is obtained for the data at each interview. With tables having more than one degree of freedom the chi-square statistic is often of limited value since it merely indicates that somewhere in the table there are data that depart from a chance distribution, but it does not locate that departure within the table. It can therefore be something of a blunt instrument. In the present case, however, there is little doubt as to where the discrepancy lies and the pattern is the same for each of the three tables.

Amongst drug users who have agency contact, the discourse is dominated to an extremely high degree by types three and four. By contrast, those who are not in agency contact show a broader spread of discourses across categories, but with a clear tendency for types one and two to be the most common. Furthermore, type five positive (5+) is only produced by a small number of respondents, mostly from the treatment group. Since 5+ is regarded as a successful outcome within the confines of the model, this suggests that during the course of the study most subjects were caught in a 3/4 subcycle, with relatively few making the escape into 5+. Out of 454 *interviews* (i.e. not independent subjects) conducted with people in agency contact, only 16 (3.5%) produced type 5+ discourse.

A number of important papers by authors such as Katz and Singh (1986), Eiser *et al.* (1985), Eiser and Gossop (1979), Gossop *et al.* (1982), Grove (1993), Eiser and van der Pligt (1986), Jenks (1994) and many others have shown how beliefs about addiction, addicted styles of attribution, or styles of attribution characterised by stable/uncontrollable attributions, are associated with failure to quit. One of the more notable approaches to this issue can be found in Eiser and van der Pligt *(op. cit.)* in which a path analysis is used to create a model capable of predicting attempts to cut down or stop smoking. The model strongly implicates a stability factor as an important mediator of intention to quit, and data from an attribution questionnaire suggest that those who saw themselves as more addicted tended to have lower expectations of success at giving up. There is thus an existing and growing literature on this topic, and a variety of authors have found, and are still finding, that belief in one shape or form that one is "addicted" has clear implications for outcome of the type predicted by Weiner in the context of attributional studies (see Davies 1992 *op. cit.*).

With the above body of research in mind, it may be a matter for concern that so many people in contact with treatment agencies spontaneously produce addicted types of discourse which often appear to be associated with failure at quitting rather than with success. It may be worth considering to what extent particular kinds of discourse may be *required* by certain practitioners or agencies before certain services can be made available, and whether these increase or decrease the likelihood of a successful outcome at the end of the day.

Progress through the model

In the description of the model given in a previous chapter, it was suggested that there was a kind of "one way valve" between stages two and three; that entering stage three was in effect an irrevocable step (see pages 94-95.) Thereafter, a kind of innocence (stage one) is lost forever and cannot be regained, the only successful outcome goal now being stage five positive (5+). This "paradise lost"-type prediction is now examined in terms of the data obtained.

Before presenting the data on this issue, it is worth pointing out that transcripts were coded independently by judges in the following sense. Individual score sheets were identified by number only, with a separate score sheet being used for each interview. Furthermore, transcripts were ordered by time, so that sheets from the same subject were not adjacent. It was therefore impossible for any judge to know the discursive stage to which any particular respondent had been assigned at a prior interview when scoring a current one.

In Table 8a below data are presented for all subjects who were in stage 3 at the first interview, cross tabulated by their placement within the model at second and third interviews.

Table 8a

Subjects at stage three (n=120) at first interview by placement in the model at subsequent interviews.

Stage	1	2	3	4	5+	
At second interview:	0	0	56	31	2	n=89
At third interview:	1	0	17	15	2	n=35

In table 8b, similar data are presented for those who were in stage four at the first interview, cross-tabulated by their placement within the model at second and third interviews.

Table 8b

Subject at stage four (n=89) at first interview, by placement within the model at subsequent interviews.

Stage	1	2	3	4	5+	
At second interview:	0	0	14	50	1	n=65
At third interview:	0	0	10	15	0	n=25

Finally, although the numbers in cells are now getting very small, we present similar data from those who were at stage five positive (5+) at first interview in Table 8c below.

Table 8c

Subjects at stage five (n=6) at first interview, by placement within the model at subsequent interviews.

Stage	1	2	3	4	5+	
At second interview:	0	0	0	0	5	n=5
At third interview:	0	0	0	1	1	n=2

The lower n values at interviews subsequent to that specified at the head of each table are due to failures of re-contact (e.g. in Table 8c, there were six subjects in stage 5+ at first interview. At second interview, five of these were re-contacted. At third interview, two were re-contacted, and so on).

The data in the above tables do not warrant any detailed inferential statistical analysis (there are virtually no data points in stages 1 and 2) since the issues to be raised are straightforward and may be seen from simple observation. With the proviso that due to failures of re-contact some caution is warranted in interpreting the results, the conclusions appear to be as follows. Firstly, examination of those at stages three, four and five of the model at initial interview shows that only one subject from among those re-contacted moved from any of those stages to the initial stages (one and two) of the model throughout the duration of the project. The prediction that such movement cannot occur is therefore strongly supported by these data, with only a single exception. Whilst it may be that such movement may occur in extremely rare circumstances (upon which our data can shed no light), as exemplified by the fact that such movement did occur in one case, we feel it is reasonable to assert that to all intents and purposes the "one way valve" postulated between stages two and three has been demonstrated. In the absence of strong contrary data, we suggest that this be taken as a working and testable property of this model as it operates within our own particular societal context.

The data also show that numbers of people moved from stage three to four, but there was also a noticeable trend in the opposite direction. On the other hand relatively few made the transition from four to five positive (5+). Thus Table 8a shows numbers of people moving from stage three to stage four; and Table 8b, which shows the future destinations of those who were initially at stage 4, shows that *virtually all of those who moved* from this box went back to stage 3. This evidence of to-and-fro movement between stages 3 and 4 suggests that these stages might represent a sub-cycle within which particular individuals can become enmeshed, rotating around these two stages perhaps for considerable periods, or perhaps indefinitely, without ever escaping into box 5+. If such were the case, it would appear that a cycle centring around treatment and treatment breakdown has been identified, each stage of which has its own characteristic and recognisable "story".

Individual predictors of change

During the coding of transcripts, judges had been encouraged to make a prediction as to the stage each subject would be in at the next interview (see Fig 3, question 16). Analysis of these data produced results that seemed hard to believe, with extremely high levels of significance being achieved from contingency tables having strong diagonals. This proved to be artefactual; judges rated many clients at each stage as unlikely to change, and many clients did not in fact change. Predicting "no change" was thus in probabilistic terms a safe strategy, which yielded high levels of significance principally because no prediction of change had in fact been made, and none had taken place. In order to examine this more closely, we repeated the analysis after removing all subjects who stayed at the same stage at successive interviews, but the problem was not solved. Now we had high degrees of significance arising from the high number of near misses; that is errors involving just one category. Subjects who changed tended to change by only one stage, so the high number of near misses was still a consequence of "same" ratings by judges. Subjects who moved simply departed from these "same" ratings by one category, giving spuriously high degrees of significance once more. These problems proved insuperable given the existing data base, and this line of thinking was abandoned. If prediction of change was to prove possible, a more detailed method was required.

In a further attempt to shed light on the feasibility of predicting transition between stages at an individual level, Maria Crugeira and Linda Wright devised a rather clever form of analysis which shed a degree of illumination on the problem. They proposed taking people at a particular stage *at time* 'a', and partitioning this group into two subgroups according to whether they stayed in that stage or moved to an adjacent designated stage, at time 'b'. Their discourses at time 'a' were then analysed by looking for statistically significant differences between the groups in terms of the underlying dimensional scores. For example, in one of these analyses we selected all stage 3s at *initial* interview. This group was then partitioned into those who in fact remained in stage 3 at the next interview, and those who moved on to stage 4. We then looked at the initial interview transcripts for these people to see if there were any detectable differences between initial stage 3 transcripts that subsequently *stayed* at stage 3, and the initial transcripts of those who subsequently moved into stage 4.

There are strengths and weaknesses to this form of analysis. Firstly, there can be no question of contamination or coding bias since Crugeira and Wright proposed an analysis that predicted future change on the basis of transcript data collected and coded at a time when the next round of data did not yet exist. On the other hand, the weakness with the analysis proposed arises from the increased likelihood of type-one errors that results when large numbers of independent significance tests are carried out. In the present case, we examined movement from stage 2 to 3, from stage 3 to 4, from stage 4 to 3 (i.e. movement backwards within the model, of the type observed in the previous analysis) using data from first and second interviews. Small numbers in cells precluded meaningful analysis of other possible comparisons. Since each comparison involved the dimensions of purposiveness, hedonism, generalisability, time, three species of reductionism, addiction and contradictoriness, the analysis involved 9 x 3 comparisons from which 6 emerged as statistically significant at $p = 0.05$ (Mann Whitney) or better. Since at this level of significance, one would expect 5 significant results per 100 comparisons due to chance, there is a strong possibility that 2 (actually 1.35) of the significant results we obtained are due to accidents and errors of sampling and procedure.

It remains to say that in statistical terms the results are less than satisfactory since we have no way of deciding which of the significant results is likely to be real, and which due to chance factors. Furthermore, numbers of "movers" in stage 1, and also at the later interviews (due to sample attrition) were sometimes very small, so a thorough analysis covering all interviews and all stages was not carried out. However, we used two-tailed tests throughout, although we could have presented a stronger picture by claiming an *a priori* basis for the use of one-tailed tests. With these caveats, we believe the analysis provides glimpses of the possible dynamics of change between stages. In every case where a significant difference was found, it was in the direction predicted by the theoretical model outlined in the previous chapter, and therefore makes a compelling degree of sense which is difficult to dismiss despite the statistical caveats. As mentioned above, six significant differences were found, and these are detailed in table 9 below. Also included is a variable which achieved marginal significance.

Table 9

Dimensions within baseline scripts which predicted change between stages at subsequent interview. (Mann Whitney)

Change from stage 2 to stage 3 (First to second interviews)
physiological reductionism $p = 0.039$

Change from stage 3 to stage 4 (First to second interviews)
hedonism $p = 0.004$
contradictoriness $p = 0.005$
purposiveness $p = 0.017$
time $p = 0.058)$

Change from stage 4 to stage 3 (First to second interviews)
generalisability $p = 0.016$
hedonism $p = 0.041$

If we now consider the above results in the light of the proposed model, certain striking features emerge. Those who moved from stage 2 into stage 3 were more likely to make use of physiological reductionism in their discourses than were those who stayed in stage 2 (5 out of 7 "movers" showed this discursive trait, whilst only 2 out of 10 "non-movers" showed it). No other dimensions showed a significant difference; a point which will be discussed again in a later section.

Movement from stage three to four was more clearly signalled in terms of three (possibly four) dimensions. Examination of the data shows that shows that 50 out of 56 "non-movers" fell in the categories low or quite low for hedonism whereas the hedonism scores of "movers" were less polarised with 12 out of 31 scoring in the mid-point of the scale ("mixed") or "quite high"; contradictoriness scores were low for non-movers (50 out of 56 scoring contradictoriness absent) whilst movers were more likely to show such signs (11 out of 31); purposiveness was "quite low" or "low" for all 56 "non-movers" whereas there were more signs of purposiveness in the moving group (7 out of 31 scoring mixed or high purposiveness); and finally the marginal result for time reveals that 37 out of 56 "non-movers" gave explanations for drug use based wholly in the past, whereas only 14 from 31 "movers" gave such an explanation. To summarise the preceding paragraph, in comparison with people who remained in the same stage, people who moved from stage three to four were more likely to show signs of hedonism, contradictoriness, and purposiveness, and were less likely to explain their drug use purely in terms of past events, during their previous interview.

Backward movement from stage 4 to stage 3 was signalled by two dimensions, namely generalisability and hedonism. In terms of generalisability, subjects who moved from stage four back to three produced responses covering the top three categories of the (five point) scale (n=14) whereas those remaining at stage four occupied the bottom four categories. The most notable distinction between the groups was the failure of "movers" to score "low" or "quite low" on this scale, coupled with the failure of non-movers to score "high". In terms of hedonism, the data are less clear cut but the contingency table shows movers as being mode likely to score "mixed" or "quite low" (7 out of 14) whilst non-movers are more likely to score from "mixed" to the top of the scale (39 out of 50). To summarise, those who moved from stage four back to stage three tended to show a return to broadly based (general) explanations for their drug use, and showed signs of a decrease in hedonism.

Overall, therefore, we can conclude that there are signs of change and direction of change detectable in the initial transcripts of those who subsequently do change. These signs are not obvious, and the picture is incomplete. On the other hand, the significant results are *without exception in the direction predicted by the model* this applies not only to progress through the model but also to backward movement from stage four to stage three, where an opposite pattern of dimensional change is predicted and obtained. The evidence thus suggests that the model works in both directions. Finally, these signs of change are detectable in transcripts obtained prior to change taking place, and in that sense are real-time predictions.

Although there are a number of statistical caveats that need to be borne in mind, the fact that in every instance where significant dimensional change takes place, that change accords with the predictions of the model, makes these findings difficult to dismiss.

Subjects entering treatment during the course of the study

A key question concerning the proposed functional discursive model is the point at which hedonistic and volitional discourses which characterise the early stages of the model give way to type three addicted discourse. A number of speculations concerning this issue arise at point of entry into treatment. It has been suggested elsewhere that in certain treatment settings, addicted discourse of type three may be mutually reinforcing for both the therapist/counsellor and his/her client. Furthermore, on the basis of attributional studies, Davies (1992 *op. cit.*) argued that repeated rehearsal of certain types of explanation can eventually translate into behaviour. In a sense, the repeated definition of self in terms of a stereotype of helpless addiction increases the likelihood (or in some circumstances even requires?) that stereotyped addicted behaviour will be produced. An important question which arises from this idea thus concerns the relationship between client and therapist, and the direction of dominant influence so far as the addiction stereotype is concerned. Does the therapist initiate addicted discourse, or does the client?

During the course of the study, 49 subjects who were not in agency contact at time 1 subsequently entered into treatment or agency contact. Examination of the data from this group at interview one (prior to engagement with treatment) shows that the majority had already adopted stage three "drugspeak". Table 10 below shows the initial distribution over the stages of the model of those whose subsequently came into treatment or agency contact later in the study.

Table 10

Discursive stage at initial interview of those who subsequently came into treatment or agency contact during the study.

Stage	1	2	3	4	5+
	0	4	30	15	0

The data show that no-one from stage one came into agency contact/treatment during the course of the study. This is perhaps not surprising unless one views recreational drug use as an inevitable precursor to addiction. The distribution over stages two and three is more interesting however. If a predominance of type twos were to be observed at initial contact, this would suggest that the act of entry into treatment might be instrumental in initiating type three discourse; we have seen in a previous table how those in treatment provide addicted or post-addicted discourse to the virtual exclusion of all else. However, in the present case type two discourse is completely dominated by type three. The data thus suggest that those who subsequently entered treatment had already adopted addicted types of discourse prior to that event. Whilst we may argue that addicted discourse meets the needs of both client and therapist in many circumstances, and that in a sense some therapists may even require such discourse in order to pursue certain anticipated courses of action, there is no basis here for the suggestion that the therapists and counsellors in the present study directly engendered this type of discourse. What we can say, however, is that those who subsequently entered treatment had already made the transition, and that the treatment group was almost exclusively drawn from amongst those who had done so.

The data in Table 11 below reinforce this point further. The top line of the table gives the discursive stage for all those who were not in agency contact at first (time one) interview. The second line then gives the figures by discursive stage for those who never came into agency contact during the study.

Table 11

Subjects not in agency contact at time one, and subjects who never came into agency contact, by discursive stage.

Stage	1	2	3	4	5
Not in agency contact at time one	27	22	33	19	0
Never in agency contact	27	18	3	4	0

The figures in the above table show that a group of 27 subjects displaying type 1 discourse at first interview remained intact, with no agency contact over the 18-month period of data collection. For type 2 discourse, the initial group of 22 was eroded slightly to 18. By contrast, the erosion of the groups, not in agency contact at first interview, but displaying type 3 or type 4 discourses was little short of catastrophic, with the vast majority of these coming into agency contact during the course of the study.

At risk of sounding scurrilous, it is suggested that there may exist a phenomenon which is a logical counterpart to the notion of "denial". The notion of "denial", a situation in which a patient insists that he/she does not have a problem when they in fact do, implies the existence of a reciprocal idea, namely that of "false affirmation" whereby the client insists they have a problem when they don't. It remains only to add that from a functional discursive perspective it is not difficult to conceive of situations in which false affirmation would be advantageous and/or reinforcing. However, we have no data on our individual clients with which to test such a hypothesis.

Street drugs and discursive stages

The next thing we examined was the pattern of relationships between use of specific drugs and discursive stage of the model. Does a particular type of discourse predict use of certain drugs rather than others? In order to answer this question, we first deleted from the analysis all drugs that were coded as "prescribed". This is particularly important for the methadone and minor tranquillisers, since a relationship here between type of drug use and discursive stage could be spurious, and arise due to the fact that those in treatment tend to produce type three discourse (see above) and would also be most likely to receive methadone and tranquillisers as part of that treatment. The data reported below are thus specific to non-prescribed street drugs.

For each drug reported we computed the numbers who claimed using it and the numbers who did not, in each stage of the model. Then a chi-square value was computed on the basis of the raw scores. We repeated this analysis for interviews one and two, but not for interview three as numbers in cells precluded further inferential analysis. Table 12 below shows the profile for each drug that yielded a significant chi-square at either interview. The data in the table are expressed as percentages of those at each stage who used the drug rather than raw scores, as this makes it easier to evaluate the overall profiles for each drug. Drugs that were mentioned that did not produce significant chi-square values at either interview comprised DF 118, cocaine, temgesic (buprenorphine), solvents, and diazepam.

Table 12

Type of drug use by discursive stage: percentage of users in each stage of the model.

Stage	1	2	3	4	5+	chi-square (based on raw drug use scores)
Drug name.						
Alcohol (1)	63	30	20	15	50	p less than 0.0001
Alcohol (2)	63	33	11	8	50	p less than 0.0001
Heroin (1)	3	37	21	29	17	p = 0.017
Heroin (2)	16	17	23	24	25	p = n.s.
Methadone (1)	0	3	15	25	0	p = 0.002
Methadone (2)	0	8	21	16	0	p = 0.113 n.s.
Temazepam (1)	10	27	29	44	17	p = 0.007
Temazepam (2)	26	0	32	40	12	p = 0.047
Cannabis (1)	90	63	27	33	33	p less than 0.0001
Cannabis (2)	90	75	15	26	12	p less than 0.0001
LSD (1)	47	17	0	7	0	
LSD (2)	42	17	0	1	0	sig?
Ecstasy (1)	23	27	2	9	0	p less than 0.0001
Ecstasy (2)	26	25	0	6	0	p less than 0.0001
Speed (amphet) (1)	50	37	7	21	33	p less than 0.0001
Speed (amphet) (2)	47	58	3	16	12	p less than 0.0001

Footnote: sample size (n) for the stages is as follows. For interviews one, stage 1 = 30, stage 2 = 30, stage 3 = 120, stage 4 = 89, stage 5 = 6. For interview two, stage 1 = 19, stage 2 = 12, stage 3 = 75, stage 4 = 83, stage 5 = 8.

In interpreting the above data, it should be mentioned that the 'n' for stage 5 is unacceptably low in statistical terms at both interviews. Also, use of percentages to describe numbers less than

100, though commonplace, is a contradiction in terms. The footnote to the previous page provides details of the 'n' in each case.

The first impression from the table is that use of some drugs appears to cluster towards the central and later stages of the model, whilst a different subset clusters in the initial stages.

Stage three and four discourse seems to characterise most methadone users. The reader should bear in mind that the above table refers solely to reported use of street drugs. The strong tendency for those in treatment to produce type three discourse accounts partly for the association between type three discourse and prescribed methadone use. However, the data in Table 12 above indicate that an association between use of methadone and a particular form of self presentation extends also to street (non-prescribed) methadone. Further analysis of the data shows how this probably comes about. At interview 1 there were 41 subjects who reported use of methadone. Of these, 31 were already in agency/treatment contact. Only one street methadone user in our sample reported no agency contact. The street methadone users were therefore people already in treatment, or who were shortly to enter treatment; and this suggests that use of street methadone was largely a continuation of treatment services. Although the individual data to support the specific point are not available, it seems reasonable to speculate on the basis of the above that in our sample street methadone use was largely confined to those receiving prescribed methadone, "topping up" their prescriptions. The low prevalence of reports of street methadone use by those with no agency contact throughout the study suggests that the problem of street methadone may be largely caused by those in treatment who receive what they take to be an insufficient supply.

Finally with respect to methadone, the fact that the type-three/type-four cycle appears to locate most of their discourses may be important if the use of therapeutic methadone is assumed to promote a period of stability during which some form of psychological reappraisal/behavioural change takes place. In our study, no methadone user managed to move into box 5+. On the contrary; the data are consistent with the observations of some drug workers that methadone *per se* may be seen as a "badge" of addiction. For some users it may legitimate the "helpless addict" stereotype and "fix" the user in an unproductive subcycle of the model. This may have a bearing on the problem of clients retained for long periods on methadone without any psychological reappraisal or behavioural change taking place.

Methadone resembles heroin to some extent in that users frequently produce stage 3 and stage 4 types of discourse. However, it differs importantly in that whereas for methadone there appears to be no hedonistic stage 1 discourse, and very little stage two, there are important numbers of heroin users at stages 1 and 2 suggesting the possibility of volitional, non-addicted and hedonistic heroin use of a type that makes stage 1 and stage 2 discourse a reasonable mode of self presentation. This group do not present themselves as "addicts". In a similar way, there is marginal evidence for the existence of a group of stage 5+ heroin users who have achieved a non-addicted pattern of use once more, after having been through the earlier "addicted" stages of the model. This may be an important difference between heroin discourses and methadone discourses; namely, there were no methadone discourses based on hedonism and volition, and no post-addiction methadone discourses. Both of these were present for heroin. Lastly with respect to heroin, there are similarities between it and the temazepam profile. Whilst the bulk of temazepam discourse occurs in stages 3 and 4 (the data are not independent; many subjects used both heroin and temazepam) there is also non-addicted temazepam discourse in stages 1 and 2, suggesting there may be different patterns of temazepam use, both volitional/hedonistic/non-addicted, and a more dependent style based on the stage 3 addiction discourse; as with heroin.

The next most striking feature from table 12 is the presence of a pair of drugs which produce to some degree an opposite picture to that presented by heroin and methadone. LSD and ecstasy discourses seem for the most part to occupy the earlier stages of the model, and to be absent or rare in the later stages. This is consistent with their characterisation as recreational drugs, and with research evidence that a subculture and a set of self perceptions surrounds their use which tends to differ from the "addicted" discourse of heroin and methadone users. The data also show that whilst numbers of LSD and ecstasy users enter into stage 2, a stage associated with awareness of problems and the need for contradictory types of self-presentation, only a small proportion of these become involved in situations within which "addicted" types of discourse become functional. The numbers is stages 3 and 4 are low. If these are indeed the "gateway" drugs which have been suggested, it is not apparent from this analysis.

Finally, there are some intriguing resemblances between the profiles of the alcohol, speed (amphetamine) and cannabis discourses.

Like ecstasy and LSD, there are substantial numbers of stage 1 and stage 2 discourses from users of all these three drugs with the modal discourse appearing to be stage 1 followed by stage 2. However, there are also considerable numbers appearing in stages 3 and 4. It appears that, particularly for cannabis and alcohol, virtually any type of discourse can emerge with at least some regularity. This may be due to the fact that many subjects, regardless of stage or the nature of their drug habit, used cannabis and/or alcohol as an adjunct to that habit; cannabis thus does not form part of an identifiable sub-pattern of drug use but can "fit in" almost anywhere. The same may be true for speed, though there is a relative absence of type 3 discourse for these users. As a consequence, setting aside the probable fact that most people who *only* use cannabis tend to produce type 1 discourse, it remains paradoxically true to say that by virtue of the ability of cannabis to accompany virtually any type of drug habit, its ability to predict stage 1 unproblematic drug use appears, on the basis of these data, to be rather less than that of ecstasy or LSD. By contrast, amongst drug users, use of these latter two drugs seems to be the best predictor of non-problematic reports of drug use.

It remains only to say that the alcohol data show in fairly clear form a regular progression in terms of numbers from stage to stage. As mentioned earlier, these data are difficult to interpret since they include subjects for whom alcohol was the primary problem substance. The profile differs from most of the other substances, with the exception of cannabis.

Methadone use by the clinical group

In the above section, there was some discussion about the use of street methadone, and the types of discourse associated with its use. The point was made that type 1 and type 5+ discourses were totally absent with respect to this drug. It seemed likely however that this was at least in part due to the fact that most of the users of street methadone belonged to a group who were in agency or treatment contact, and whose discourse was dominated by types 3 and 4 in any case. In order to shed more light on this phenomenon we examined more closely methadone use in the clinical group, focusing specifically on prescribed methadone. As in previous analyses, we examined data for the three different rounds of data collection. We also grouped subjects according to the amount prescribed, grouping clinical subjects into those with high dose methadone (the upper tertile), medium dose (the middle tertile), low dose (the bottom tertile) and those with no prescription for methadone. Table 13 below shows the results of this analysis, when the above groups are cross tabulated by discursive stage.

Table 13

Clinical group; amount of prescribed methadone by discursive stage.

Time 1.

Stage	1	2	3	4	5	
high dose	0	0	10	9	1	
medium dose	0	0	11	10	0	
low dose	0	0	12	9	0	
none (zero) prescribed	1	7	2	6	1	p less than 0.0003

Time 2.

Stage	1	2	3	4	5	
high dose	0	0	8	11	1	
medium dose	0	0	13	7	0	
low dose	0	0	8	13	0	
none (zero)	1	2	4	7	1	p = 0.07 (n.s.)

Time 3.

Stage	1	2	3	4	5	
high dose	0	0	5	6	0	
medium dose	0	0	6	5	0	
low dose	0	0	4	7	0	
none (zero) prescribed	2	0	3	3	1	p = 0.18 (n.s.)

The above data are shown to be statistically significant only at time 1. However, the high number of zeros at stages 1, 2 and 5 means that the significance is based almost entirely on entries in columns 3 and 4. Consequently, the significant result at time 1 derives mainly from the low numbers at stages 3 and 4 for those not on a methadone prescription. The non-significant results in the other two cases derive mainly from the fact that the distribution of results at stages 3 and 4 does not depart significantly from chance. Overall therefore we may cautiously conclude that type of discourse probably bears no relationship to prescribed dose. If it does, however, it only affects those receiving no prescription in the sense that they produce fewer examples of addicted discourse. Finally, we can see from the tables that non-addicted discourses of types 1 and 2 were only ever produced by those receiving no methadone prescription; and that the small number of type 5+ discourses that occurred came from people with either no methadone prescription, or a high dose prescription. The most striking feature of these data however remains the concentration of those receiving prescribed methadone in discursive stages 3 and 4, largely independent of dose. A possible interpretation of these data is that prescribed methadone *per se,* largely independently of quantity, is indeed seen as a drug that endorses and in some sense legitimates "addiction". If such is the case, it is possible that methadone is a factor in fixing some people in the repeated stage 3/stage 4 subcycle identified in an earlier section. At risk of oversimplifying, a possible summary of the methadone data overall (i.e. both prescribed and non-prescribed) might be, "no-one is having fun and hardly anyone is getting better".

As a footnote to this section, there are intriguing preliminary reports from Portugal, where Crugeira is currently collecting cross-national data on the five-stage model. It appears that naloxone, an opiate antagonist (methadone is an opiate agonist that mimicks certain actions of opiates; antagonists do the opposite), is the preferred drug of maintenance at many sites in Portugal. She reports tantalisingly that the early indications are that those on prescribed naloxone exhibit the same pattern of dependent and addicted discourse that is manifested by methadone users in our own society, despite the fact that the pharmacology of the two drugs in question is basically opposite in action. However, data collection is still under way, so time will tell whether these early impressions are subsequently borne out.

Counsellors'/therapists' ratings, and the five-·stage model

The final part of the analysis involved an attempt to relate aspects of the discursive model to confidential ratings of clients made by their counsellors and therapists. Towards the end of the study, we contacted counsellors and therapists and asked if they would be willing to fill in a short confidential pro-forma describing the situation they felt clients were currently facing. The pro-forma comprised a series of questions concerning improvement, stability or deterioration in the drug related behaviour of clients. This proved a difficult task, with some therapists and counsellors being unwilling to undertake the task, whilst others failed to do so for a variety of reasons. At the end of the day, pro-formas were completed on 84 clients by 21 different therapists, with 11 of the forms being unattributable to a particular therapist. The pro-forma used in the study sought information on 11 different aspects of drug related behaviour, as follows:

1. Client identification.
2. Therapist identification.
3. Length of client contact.
4. Is client still in contact?
5. Change in level of street drug use.
6. Change in level of prescription.
6a. Reason for such change.
7. Change in frequency of injection.
8. Change in level of drug-related criminality.
9. Overall assessment of functioning (e.g. stable, improving, getting worse).
10. Any other comments.

Analysis proceeded by cross-tabulating the clinicians' responses against discursive stage. Since the therapists' ratings were collected at the end of the study, clients' discursive stage at the last interview was used as the criterion.

An important feature of the proposed five-stage discursive model should be its ability to demonstrate that clients who improve over time move to discursive stages that are functionally different from those occupied by clients who do not improve. For example, stage three improvers ought to move into stage four since this is seen as a necessary step on the way to 5+; and stage four improvers ought to move to stage 5+ (though we may note from previous analyses that this may be difficult to demonstrate, since very few subjects of any description in fact made that transition). By contrast, those whose condition deteriorates ought to move from the later stages back into stage 3. Earlier analyses have in fact demonstrated that change of this type does take place. However, in order to test this prediction of the model further, the above data obtained from therapists and counsellors were now used as the benchmark against which to test the hypothesis. The hypothesis was tested independently for each variable on which therapists/counsellors provided data, by cross tabulating those data against the discursive stage of the model in which the client appeared at the last interview. It remains only to say that the results of these analyses were disappointing. Whilst there were small numbers of improvers in certain cells who appeared to support the theory, the power-house of the model from a treatment perspective is stages 3 and 4, and the overall distribution of improvers, non-improvers and deteriorators over these cells never departed from chance. Only one variable produced results which bordered on statistical significance (p = .08). and this concerned changes to clients' prescriptions. Strangely even this highly marginal result did not produce clear evidence to support the theory. Increased prescriptions had been provided to seven stage 3 clients, but to only two stage 4 clients; but a majority of stage 4 clients were on constant rather than reducing prescriptions; and an agreed reduction seemed equally likely in either stage 3 or 4. We have to conclude therefore that for the clinical subjects for whom therapists' reports were obtained, no changes in discursive style were detectable that could be said to underscore therapists' assessments of client progress.

The above results are disappointing, but not fatal. There are a number of ways in which the methodology of the study as designed proved less than ideal for testing this hypothesis. Perhaps the model requires more subtle assessment methods in order to discriminate between the two key stages, 3 and 4. Perhaps therapists use criteria for their assessments that differ from the assumptions on which the model is based. For example, a move from stage 3 to 4 is seen as a necessary step towards 5+ in terms of the model, but may also be construed as 'relapse' by those with a different theoretical orientation.

In a final attempt to shed light on this issue we tried to discover whether there was any consensus about clients' improving or deteriorating status between therapists' assessments and our own assessments based on the coding of transcripts. We examined all of the criteria used by therapists, and in each case we cross-tabulated these against increased, stable, or decreased use of street drugs as coded from transcripts by our judges. It remains merely to say that overall the picture that emerged was very confused, with no statistically defensible conclusion being possible. Table 14 below represents the type of picture that repeatedly emerged. In table 14, therapists' ratings of their clients in terms of the categories 'marked improvement', 'slight improvement', 'no change' and 'deterioration' are cross tabulated against our own ratings of street drug use. These latter are categorised into 'increase', 'constant', 'decrease' and 'stopped' on the basis of comparisons of reported street drug use *between interviews* in other words, our own scale is time based, and derived by comparing fluctuations in reported drug use between consecutive interviews.

Table 14

Therapists' ratings by changes in reported street drug use.

	marked improvement	slight improvement	no change	deterioration
increase	5	9	11	4
constant	7	9	3	1
decrease	6	12	9	3
stopped	1	3	1	0

The distribution of data across the cells does not depart significantly from chance; a disappointing pattern found in all other cases with respect to this analysis. What we can note, however, is that therapists found an improvement, either marked or slight in 52 of the 84 clients. This improvement, however, was not related in any significant way to changes in pattern of reported street drug use, though 35 respondents were in fact coded as showing a decrease or cessation in street drug use between interviews. In a similar way, we can say that 24 clients were rated as 'no change' by their therapists, and 20 as 'constant' on our own measure of street drug use. However, whilst there may be some apparent pattern of similarity in these overall numbers, the low chi-square value for the table (p = .65 n.s.) indicates clearly that such agreement does not extend to agreement about individuals. For example, whilst therapists identified 24 as 'no change' in terms of street drug use, only three of these occur at the correct intersection in the data matrix. It is clear that whilst the two data sets may show surface similarities in terms of numbers identified as belonging to certain categories, there is no agreement in terms of who belongs in those categories.

In a way similar to that described above, we examined all the other variables rated by therapists, with very similar results. In no case was there statistically robust evidence of a relationship between therapists' ratings and changes in street drug use as coded by ourselves on the basis of between-interview comparisons. It is of course eminently reasonable to propose that improvement or deterioration can involve many things other than extent of street drug use, and that therapists' ratings might well have been based on other criteria. At this stage we restrict our conclusions therefore merely to the statement that therapists' assessments on all fronts bore little relationship to our measure of change of street drug use. However, this conclusion extends also to therapists' own ratings of clients' street drug use, which once again bore little or no relationship to our own measure derived from comparison of reports of drug use between interviews (therapists' assessment of street drug use x research assessment of street drug use: p = .19 n.s. chi square for 12 D.F.).

Lest our therapists feel badly served by these data, we should point out that our own assessment scores (based on a ten point scale, loosely analogous to an APGAR Score) fared no better when it came to predicting changes in street drug use.

Whilst it is necessary to concede that the data set described above fares rather badly in terms of the planned analysis, we make no apology for pursuing this matter further since the relationship between clients and their therapists, and the impressions they form of each other, are of central concern for those involved in treatment. Accordingly, at this point we shamelessly adopted a theory-free and hypothesis-free approach by using regression based statistics to trawl through the data in the hope that something might be dredged from the sea bed that might warrant some *post hoc* comment. (Regression based data dredging is generally a poor way of doing research; we would argue however that it might be excused in some circumstances provided it is only seen as a way a generating possible hypotheses for future testing rather than as a way of 'proving' *ex post facto* hypotheses.) Accordingly we decided to look at the pattern of intercorrelations between our own global assessment ratings, therapists' overall assessment ratings, our own criteria for street drug use, and therapists' ratings of street drug use. The pattern proves interesting. Firstly, the correlation (Spearman) between our own global assessment of client progress, and therapists' assessment, was negative (rho = -32, p = .003). We were clearly not doing the same thing. It is possible that part of this apparent anomaly was due to the fact that stage 4 discourse might be seen by some therapists as a negative or relapse stage, whereas within our own framework this would be seen as a necessary stage in the road to recovery.*

---

*We are encouraged in this interpretation by a paper about smoking cessation from DiClemente and Prochaska (1985 *op. cit.*) who write (page 339) "Instead of seeing relapse as failure, smoking control programs should help relapsers consolidate and direct their coping efforts towards reentry into the cycle of change." In the study cited, 27% of relapsers entering the study were not smoking two years later, compared to only 11.5% of "contemplators".

Unfortunately, our existing data are insufficiently fine grained to shed light on this possibility. Secondly, our own assessment of client progress correlated 0.26 (p = 0.02) with our own measure of street drug use; and 0.19 (n.s.) with therapists' ratings of street drug use. Thus our own assessments showed rather small but nonetheless positive correlations with both measures of street drug use. Thirdly, therapists' assessments correlated negatively (-0.07 n.s.) with our measure of street drug use; and amazingly negatively (-0.55 ; p less than 0.001) with *their own* assessment of street drug use. If such a pattern of data were to emerge from a more focused study into this issue, certain possible implications might be derived. It would appear, for example, that whatever the therapists achieved with their clients (or believed they had achieved) was at best independent of their clients reported drug use, or at worst actually negatively associated with such use.

It is worth reiterating that our own system of coding was 'blind', since our measure of street drug use was only derived after all data had been collected, at which point successive interviews were compared in order to derive the measure of improvement, stability, or deterioration. This categorisation was thus not available to those coding the transcripts'. By contrast, therapists' ratings were not 'blind', since both ratings were made on the same data sheet. A need is clearly signalled here for a study into client improvement/deterioration, into the criteria that therapists and counsellors use in arriving at assessments of client progress, and the psychological and interpersonal factors that influence therapists' ratings. Whatever the facts of the matter, there are clearly serious gaps in our understanding of how the client/therapist relationship works, and how impressions of client progress are formed.

If anything emerges from these analyses it concerns a slight but consistent bias in terms of the aggregate data. In all the above analyses therapists and counsellors assigned larger numbers to 'improved' or 'better' categories than were similarly assigned by our own 'change in street drug use' criterion. This may indicate a slight but consistent degree of optimism on the part of therapists; if so, that is probably no bad thing.

9

Conclusions

The relative merits of strongly cued and minimally cued data

In a previous chapter considerable consideration was given to the issue of social criterion, the idea that a subject's criterion for saying one thing rather than another varies according to circumstances, in the same way that subjects' statements about sensory responses vary in a signal detection experiment. Within that same chapter, an analogy was also drawn between the degree of cueing implicit in the method of choice, and the notion of signal strength. In our own study, described in the previous chapter, we tried to adopt an interviewer style that would be non-threatening and which would therefore require fewer defensive "addiction" explanations; this is standard practice in many studies, and represents as far as many researchers are able to go in ensuring the "truthfulness" of subjects' answers. Such an approach, coupled with a guarantee of anonymity or confidentiality, is assumed to remove the motivation to tell other than the truth. However, we also employed a minimally cued method that would allow respondents to elaborate on their own salient themes, rather than be constrained by the researchers' salient themes. We can say in advance that the data produced by such a method are likely to be less comprehensive than is normally felt desirable in standard questionnaire studies, since they are selective and based on a set of saliences coming from the individual, rather than from the researcher. By contrast, the questionnaire or survey researcher requires his/her questionnaire or interview schedule to be as comprehensive as possible with respect to the data base envisaged; and consequently, numbers of issues are cued (and thus require a response) which might not have arisen otherwise. In signal detection terms, these two contrasting methods are seen as analogous to conditions which produce on the one hand fewer hits and fewer false positives, and on the other hand conditions which produce more hits but more false positives. To put this in everyday terms, the highly structured, comprehensive, forced-choice type of research methodology forces similarities into the data by virtue of requiring a similar response profile from every subject. Subjects have to respond to, and hence get a score on, all the items and issues raised by the protocol. Consequently, the method suppresses subtleties of individual difference quite simply by forcing the same data framework on all subjects.

It is argued here that the standard methodology therefore actually fails to reveal certain kinds of differences between people simply because it does not allow them to occur; for example, differences arising due to omission or selection. Furthermore, there are also differences in type or quality, which may be ignored or suppressed in the interests of pursuing comparability in terms of what is assumed to be quantity. Perhaps unfortunately, the use of qualitative data has come to be associated with a particular style of selective or interpretive methodology which is seen as "unscientific" and which therefore does not meet with favour from those seeing themselves as scientists. However, we have tried to show that the use of uncued methods does not mean that one is restricted to selective interpretations of data at the expense of methodological rigour, provided a model is derived which allows the principled and replicable identification of discursive type. It is hoped that the present study goes at least some way to making that case. It is also hoped that the study described demonstrates that uncued and virtually unstructured methods can be used to find kinds of differences which are salient to clients, and which are suppressed by the researchers' agenda in the context of more structured methods. In a sense we would argue perhaps that differences can emerge between subjects not only in terms of what they say but also in terms of what they do not say; and highly structured methods have a limited capacity to shed light on those differences of omission, and only then in the most clumsy fashion. Finally, it is hoped that a methodology based on recognisable types, but making no claim to either truth or "real meaning", may satisfy the needs of "science" as currently construed by many psychologists whilst doing minimal violence to the philosophies underlying the discursive approach.

The justification for standard formats and procedures usually stems from statistical requirements rather than psychological or phenomenological considerations, and from the belief in the necessity to have comparable data from all subjects. How can one do the sums unless all subjects are measured on the same variables? Unfortunately, in some circumstances this requirement places the cart very much before the horse, since it explicitly prevents subjects from having different variable profiles. To summarise, standard formats cue standard data. But what if subjects' motives are not standardised?

It is hoped therefore that the methodology outlined in the previous chapters may in some small way indicate that useful data can be obtained from subjects by other means, and that such data can be coded in ways that are principled and replicable. It is the writer's belief that current methodologies based on philosophies of physical measurement as conceptualised in the 1930s no longer provide an adequate basis for psychological and other socially-oriented research, and that there is need for the development of alternative methodologies that take into account the constructed, functional and context-dependent nature of verbal behaviour. This suggestion goes way beyond the currently popular idea that we should all collect some qualitative data as an accompaniment to our latest questionnaire exercise, which is an unacceptable cobbling together of opposed philosophies (Davies, 1996 *op. cit.*).

Drugspeak: a life of its own?

The philosophical underpinnings of the approach described lie in the sociology of discourse, and the suggestion that the "real meaning" of an utterance can never be ascertained independently of context since its function is localised in that context. Ultimately in this writer's opinion, the philosophy of discourse is disappointing from a research perspective, since it concludes that no utterance has a "real meaning" and furthermore any suggestions as to its meaning are themselves utterances bounded by function within context. Consequently there are no expert opinions and no finality of interpretation. From such a standpoint, normative research becomes either impossible to do, or self-deluding if one does it.

We have sought to escape from this impasse by claiming the notion of motivation as the underpinning to the model, on the basis that motivation is implicit even in the writings of those who deny its existence. From that standpoint, we have dispensed with the need to decide whether any given utterance is true or not, and similarly with the need to make assertions about what a given utterance really means. We have tried to do this by concentrating entirely on conversational types, and relating these types to other things in the attempt to suggest the function they might serve. We defend our own analysis only on the basis of pragmatism, in the hope that looking at speech in this way might help solve some problems. We make no claim that our described method is true, merely that it shows promise as a usable tool. At the point where people start to ask if this last sentence can itself be, or is, "true" we merely shout *"Enough"* and refer the reader to the works of Foucault and Derrida with a recommendation that they sort out the answer to their question for themselves.

The principle hope is that the study described is sufficiently convincing to make the case that "drugspeak" has a life of its own. We have shown a developmental change in discourse as the drug user progresses through a drug using career; we have shown how discourses change as users move between stages of use; we have shown that to some extent future discursive changes are predictable on the basis of current ones; we have even shown that particular drugs are associated with their own patterns of explanation, patterns which do not simply mirror pharmacological properties or physiological states. Consequently, we wish to make a plea for counsellors, clinicians, therapists, and perhaps even politicians and news reporters, to listen more to what drug users say about their own habits and behaviour, but not simply from the standpoint of finding out what it is "really like". The plea is to listen for functions that "drugspeak" serves, and the problems it solves and creates. This is a different kind of listening.

In general terms, the things that drug users say are not treated as independent sources of useful and potentially predictive behaviour. They are seen simply as a shorthand way of finding out the way something "is", almost as though data were being retrieved from a computer; if you press the right buttons the data must come out. Thus, if you do not know what someone did last week, and you need to know, then you simply ask the right kinds of questions and they will tell you. They may choose to lie, of course, but that is a deliberate act of distortion made to conceal "the true" version which is still inside their heads. In fact of course, there is a limitless number of ways of describing what happened last week, any number of which may be said to be "true" and any number of which might be said to be "false"; consequently, there can be no principled or necessary link between a given account and "what really happened". The fact that in a questionnaire or survey many respondents may tell you the same thing is usually a consequence of the fact that they were all asked the same questions and given the same limited set of response alternatives.

Nonetheless it is sometimes observed that a given account may reflect someone else's (i.e. a consensus) version of "what really happened". This however does not undermine the fact that in principle the account and the actions have no necessary link, and come from totally different domains. Where an account appears to reflect the "facts", it does so merely because the person chooses that style of presentation because it makes sense for them to do so, just as they choose any style of presentation; regardless of whether it fits "the facts" or not. There is no principled link between the account and some reality; and if there appears to be one, it is there because someone put it there for a purpose, and that same person can modify the relationship or even take it away completely if they have reason to do so. As a result, there is really no alternative to treating verbal discourse in its own right and on its own terms, rather than merely as a quick and convenient way of measuring a person's behaviour when they are not doing it. How can we do otherwise? How can we treat such material as "scientific data" about "facts" when the link between verbal report and behaviour is dependent on the motivation of the reporter, to remove, reinstate, or reinterpret at every stage? Consequently, a pragmatically useful way of viewing drug discourse is to go beyond the surface semantics in terms of "what it means", and try instead to locate its function by asking "what does it achieve?"

The hope is that the present method may perhaps stimulate more interest in the functional and performative nature of drug discourses, hopefully at the expense of more basic formulations that still take drug discourses to be a window (albeit blurred) on the way drug use "really is". If such a viewpoint is acceptable at the outset, then it is the intention of this book to demonstrate that the contribution of verbal behaviour to the state we call "addicted" is as fundamental as pharmacological, social, individual difference, or any other variables that contribute to the state. Furthermore, such a contribution takes the form of an independent variable, rather than merely a non-independent means of accessing other independent variables. To put this another way, verbal reports communicate information in their own right by virtue of their type and function as has hopefully been demonstrated in this research; they are not simply a way of finding out other things. Consequently, a central conclusion from the research is that drugspeak has a life of its own, that certain modes of functional presentation form an integral part of the addicted state. Therefore, being "addicted" means, amongst other things, finding oneself in a situation where it is necessary to adopt certain styles of conversation in order to survive within a society that takes a particular view of certain sets of substances and imposes certain conditions, constraints and penalties on their use.

The final implication of the above is, of course, the one that may be found hardest to swallow. Consensus in the verbal reports of drug users derives from a commonality of function, not from any universal truth. This is particularly so for the non-volitional content of certain drug discourses, where an appeal to lack of volitional control serves the purpose of removing personal responsibility, blame and guilt (see Davies, 1992), rather than being a "true" report of some physiological/pharmacological internal state. From a philosophical point of view, how could a person possibly know that they were addicted? At the end of the day, the only evidence available to the individual is derived from observations of his/her own behaviour. Consequently, the verbal statement "I can't stop" is simply based on the self-observation that with some regularity I fail to do so. Least of all can it be taken as a first hand account of the workings of the brain, or a comment on the dopamine levels in the acumbens (or whatever), since there are no observations on which to base such an account. Consequently, there is no alternative to viewing drug discourses within a framework which sees language as primarily performative, rather than as primarily informative.

Elements and isotopes: useful analogy or fantasy?

The six-stage discursive model proposed in the previous chapters is not based on surface semantic themes, but on certain underlying dimensions. The assumption is that, within our own culture, similar functions will be served by each of the discursive types for all individuals within that culture and hence the model describes (in principle) all possible drug conversations it is possible to have within that cultural context. At the time of writing, a cross cultural study is being carried out by Crugeira (1996) amongst drug users in Portugal. It appears that agencies in Portugal may operate according to different principles, for example naltrexone is prescribed (an opiate antagonist) for drug users where methadone might be prescribed in our own context. Furthermore, heavy, chronic and highly problematic drug use of a type that is still relatively rare in the U.K. seems to be concentrated in a shanty district of Lisbon (for example) where users live in tiny self-constructed shacks of wood and polythene, in some numbers. The district resembles some of the shanty settlements of Brazilia and other South American cities, a social context still largely absent from the U.K. Since there is no economic support of any kind for many of these people, their natural discourses may be expected to differ from those found in inner city deprived areas of the U.K. where some standard of housing and some economic entitlement is still the norm. Their discourses *may* thus serve different purposes entirely.

Crugeira's Portuguese discourses do indeed look rather different in certain respects from the discourses which typify the model developed in the U.K. The question is, are they isotopes* of the same model, serving the same (but culturally transformed) purposes, or are they based on a model which is fundamentally different in terms of its purposes? In a previous chapter, an example of a possible Type 5- discourse (identified by the author and by Crugeira) was tentatively offered with the proviso that in the U.K. study we obtained only this single example that went beyond a brusque and usually dismissive interchange of one or two words. However, it appears that the example given has certain things in common with conversations from heavy, chronic and committed drug users in the shanties of Lisbon. This raises the question as to whether type 5- discourses are simply more common in Lisbon, or whether the Portuguese type 5- discourses are actually a small

---

*A substance is identified as a particular element on the basis of the number of protons in its nucleus; but it is identified as an isotope of that element on the basis of the number of neutrons in the nucleus.

part of a very different model. Of interest is the fact that it is non-addicted and purposive, but completely hopeless in the sense that death appears to be the future accepted outcome. At the present time, it is not clear whether the Portuguese data support a transformation (i.e. they are an isotope) of the model offered here, or whether new stages, or indeed a whole new model, is necessary.

It goes without saying that it is an exercise in idle semantics to invoke the term "isotope" unless something with practical or theoretical value emerges from such a definition. However, the exciting fact is that the analogy suggests a way of distinguishing between discourses in two different ways; namely, distinguishing between fundamentally different discursive systems underlaid by different dimensions, even if they have similar themes; and identifying as *the same* discourses which look very different in terms of semantic themes and content, but which can be identified as isotopes in terms of their underlying functional dimensions. Such a distinction is only made possible within the existing model by forms of analysis which go beyond surface content and semantic themes.

It seems likely that similarities or differences between the drug discourses of different cultures will be best revealed by methods that have the capacity to differentiate between culturally specific surface themes, preoccupations, modes of self-presentation and verbal culture, and deeper functional and performative dimensions. If the isotope analogy has any usefulness such distinctions should be possible, and in our current research we are trying to differentiate between discourses in terms of number and type of surface themes and features, and number and type of underlying functional dimensions, in two different cultures. Discourses identified as 'isotopes' should serve basically the same functions regardless of differences in their themes and appearance; on the other hand, elemental discourses should serve different functions and reflect fundamentally different culturally defined purposes, even in the face of similar thematic content.

Finally, there are other frankly mind-boggling questions to which answers, arguably, could be found. Can the theory be tested by observing what happens *when discourses collide?* Are some discourses more potent or *fissile* than others? Can some discourses start a *chain reaction* in other discourses? Do some discourses *contaminate* other discourses? Do discourses have a *half-life?* And crucially, would it be possible to use the element/isotope analogy to model these processes in ways that would have practical and useful implications?

Therapeutic possibilities

It is the belief of the author that the model described may have some usefulness in the therapeutic and clinical setting, though at the end of the day others must be the best judge of this suggestion.

The basic suggestion is that therapists view their clients discourses as indicants of current motivation, rather than as reports of actual or real events, attitudes, hopes, fears, intentions or whatever other species of "truth" we care to envisage. The two of course are not exclusive, the current framework merely offers additional possibilities. Within the proposed model, these possibilities lie at two levels, namely a) the types of discourse themselves and the situations within which they make functional sense and b) the dimensions which have been proposed as underlying the different stages, and their differential importance as contributors to those stages. The basic strategy with respect to the functional discursive model of addiction would thus involve two levels of therapeutic judgement.

Firstly, one would seek to clarify as rapidly as possible the discursive stage best characterising the client's discourse, and seek to discover the purposes it serves. Clinical judgement is then required in evaluating whether those purposes are in the client's best interests, considering the substance-use and other problems he/she is facing. The assumption is that this will often not be the case, but rather that a particular cyclical pattern of mutually reinforcing behaviour and discourse (probably involving boxes three and four) is serving to fix the client in a particular state. The danger for the therapist is that he/she inadvertently becomes part of that "fixing" process by adding external expert confirmation to short-term functional but longer-term dysfunctional cycles of explanation and behaviour. On the other hand, the therapist has the opportunity to identify a type of discourse which will better suit the clients longer term needs, or which will at least "unstick" the situation. This first stage of the process is critical, since for discourses of type one and two, and especially for younger people, the therapist may wish to consider carefully whether treatment for a substance abuse problem is appropriate at all, given the irrevocable nature of the step into discursive stage three.

Secondly, if the therapist feels that change of discursive type may be advantageous, he/she may consider the underlying dimensions for each discursive type, and seek ways of engineering change in the most salient of these according to stage. The underlying dimensions are thus the tools that one could employ in seeking to bring about a discursive change by making suggestions about cognition and behaviour that would make particular types of discourse untenable or non-functional. At this stage, it seems possible that a number of the tools already in the armoury of the cognitive/behavioural therapist and the motivational interviewer would prove especially useful. There seems in principle no reason why such techniques could not be used in the context of the proposed model.

Relapse

Two related issues arise from the data that merit specific consideration, and these concern the precise construction that is placed on box 4 discourse, and the role of the hedonism dimension in that type of discourse. It was suggested earlier that box 4 represents a discursive stage through which all clients must pass if they are to move from box 3 to box 5. It may be the case that for some clients such a passage is not possible; they fail time and time again. For such people, a twelve-step approach may be justifiable insofar as it seeks to maintain clients in box 3 indefinitely (thus, they are always "recovering"), and any move into box 4 would be seen in such a context as relapse and as undesirable. The only justification for such a therapeutic approach, however, would be that progress to discursive stage 5+ was unattainable for that particular individual.

However, in Prochaska and DiClemente's process model, alternative constructions may be placed on stages that look like "relapse". In a study of smokers for example (Prochaska & DiClemente, 1985 *op. cit. p. 338*) they write, "*Relapse... may not be as negative a consequence as has been thought. Relapsers are a very active group, often moving back into contemplating another serious attempt to quit and continuing modification activities.*" and also, "*they seem to need to continue to reevaluate themselves.... and possibly re-*

evaluate the relapse experience in order to make a more successful attempt to modify their smoking." What Prochaska and DiClemente appear to by saying is that a period during which `abstaining users' start to use (or consider using) again, may be a step on the road to a type of recovery which is impossible for those who are confined to stage 3. Whilst permanent residence in stage 3 requires the use of the epithet "I am a recovering addict" for an indefinite period, those who successfully move through box 4 and into 5+ can in a very real sense say "I used to be an addict". For some clients, therefore, it is suggested that a return to use within box 4 may be a positive rather than a negative step, if such use is underpinned by appropriate dynamics. Consequently, whether a move from "addicted" discourse to a type of discourse in which the concept of addiction starts to break down is seen in negative or positive terms, as "relapse" as opposed to "continuing recovery", depends on the underpinnings for that change. On the basis of the present argument, there is certainly no justification for seeing all such change in negative terms; and there is certainly no shortage of evidence in the clinical and social literature indicating that belief in the "addiction" construct can be an actual barrier to therapeutic progress.

Within the proposed model, stage 4 is seen as an essential step to full recovery; a stormy sea across which all those wishing or able to achieve stage 5+ must pass. Related to the above, our data suggest that the move from box 3 to box 4 discourse is accompanied by a number of things, including an increase in the amount of hedonistic reference in the discourse. This means that some subjects report a return of some of the pleasure associated primarily with box 1 discourse, when they move from box 3 into box 4. This increase in enjoyment may be of some significance, since the standard "addicted" type of discourse focuses on the use of drugs "just to keep straight". It is worth considering if the return of hedonism, and the associated increase in volition are linked in some way. It seems possible that use for pleasure might reintroduce personal motives for use into the equation in a way that might be beneficial for some individuals, since pleasure sometimes appears to bring purposiveness with it.

The above speculations may raise particular issues for methadone prescribing, if the basic philosophy of methadone rests on the idea of an opiate substitute that controls withdrawals but is not entertaining to take. This clearly raises some fairly fundamental issues, including the moral question as to how we feel about our drug addicts getting fun from their treatment! However, whilst it is beyond dispute that certain of the harms arising from uncontrolled opiate use are reduced by methadone substitution, it perhaps remains less clear that methadone maintenance therapy assists individuals to control their personal drug habit on any large scale. Whatever the truth of the matter, the data from the present study clearly indicate that methadone use, whether street or prescribed, is associated with types of discourse from which both pleasure and recovery are markedly absent. On the other hand, the role of pleasure as a factor that might influence control over a drug habit is revealed as a tantalising possibility by the discourses provided by the ecstasy and LSD users. It may be that for some individuals, a hedonistic drug habit might be incompatible with one is uncontrolled or "addicted".

Broader Issues

The broader issues raised by the present text involve the nature of the state we refer to as "addicted", and a number of the arguments mentioned here have been put forward at greater length in the previous text *The Myth of Addiction (op. cit.)*. Basically, the implications are that, although numbers of people become enmeshed in a cycle of chronic drug use, sometimes with the most serious implications for their health and for their social and economic functioning, the idea that they do so because the pharmacology of a drug or drugs removes their capacity to do otherwise is nonsensical both philosophically and empirically. It is argued that the addicted state is often misunderstood insofar as it is assumed that such compulsion is its most salient feature. Instead it is argued here that substance use and abuse is best conceived of as decision based in the same way that other complex, multi-component and planned behaviours are decision based.

Furthermore, such decisions are individually and subjectively rational in the sense that drug use "makes more sense" in some circumstances than others. A balanced and fully functional lifestyle is likely to be more "drug resistant" than one which is chaotic or non-functional for the individual. For example, there is evidence that sustained but non-addicted cocaine use is often displayed by individuals whose style of life includes other valued activities, including work, with which uncontrolled cocaine use is simply incompatible. Life styles lacking such alternative points of positive focus are less drug resistant (Harrison & Mugford, 1994). It goes without saying that wealth and opportunity are important mediators in determining whether a life style has one, or many, points of positive focus.

The evidence in support of the above conclusions comes from two sources, empirical and philosophical. It has been argued that it is a philosophical absurdity to advance a "scientific" definition of a state which has an implicit distinction between volition and determinism at its core. Any piece of behaviour has an underlying pharmacology, whether drug related or not. Consequently, specifying a mechanism for drug use cannot be used as the basis for a switch from a decision-based to a non-volitional explanation, since it is equally possible in principle to specify similar mechanisms for non drug-related actions. Volitional and non-volitional accounts of human action are alternative accounts of why people do things; one is basically existential/phenomenological in nature whilst the other is materialist/reductionist. It is difficult to envisage a useful description of any behavioural phenomenon which requires the simultaneous application of these contrasting philosophies to related aspects of the same phenomenon. To say in effect, "We will take this philosophical position on human nature when people do this, but that philosophical position when they do that," is not an act of scientific definition but is itself an illustration of the way in which people, including scientists, choose functional modes of attribution (explanation) in order to support the cases they wish to make.

It is also the hope that the present text makes the beginnings of an empirical case for viewing drug-related conversations within the broader arena of functional discourse. The things people say primarily make sense of the situations they find themselves in, and serve to make the future more tolerable and more controllable. This point has been made in a number of other publications (Davies, 1995, Davies & Best, 1995; Davies, 1996) where the variable nature of discourses is seen as attesting to their functionality-within-context, and their very variability becomes the central measure of their significance. It no longer seems reasonable to the author of this text to conceive of verbal exchanges as unmotivated attempts to describe the world "as it really is". Words are always uttered by people with motives and intentions. From such a basis, an attempt has been made to demonstrate that drug discourses serve functions which are identifiable, and a method for dealing in a principled and replicable way with minimally structured conversations has been proposed. Although all assumptions about the "truth" of these utterances were suspended, it still proved possible to develop descriptive and to some extent predictive models of discourse merely on the basis of agreement about the *type* of conversation offered. Although the method clearly needs further development, it is suggested that there is sufficient in the data to demonstrate that drugspeak has a life of its own; that it may more usefully be viewed as a central and independent component of addiction with its own dynamics, and that verbal reports are rather more than cheap and convenient indicants of how other things "really are".

Naturally, if the above account were itself "true", the implications for drug policy would differ at a number of points from policy options which are preferred at the present moment. Since the view of the public, of politicians and of the media is largely based on the unwarranted prominence that the latter reflexively (they deceive themselves as well as everyone else) give to the negative aspects of drug use, and to the lurid personal accounts of users whose habit has gone wrong and who have come to public attention, we can expect a set of policy options which fail to confront the real issues of drug use in our own contemporary society. Instead of a set of adaptive coping responses, we continue to pursue wars on drugs whose function is not to cope (this is described as "condoning drug use" in the rhetoric of drug wars) but to pursue the impossible dream of stamping out drugs from our midst. The saddest thing however is that the whole edifice is based on a misconception about what people are actually doing when they talk about, describe, and above all explain, their drug use. Whereas drug warriors see their efforts as a moral reaction to the horrors of compulsive and addicted drug use, which must be stamped out by whatever means are necessary, it can be argued that the causal chain is if anything the other way round. The data from the present study suggest that the self-fulfilling, non-volitional and helpless accounts of drug users may well be functional adaptations to the demand characteristics and the legal and social sanctions favoured by the drug warriors themselves. They have survival value in a hostile environment. And so we have a perfect, self-energising and totally inappropriate system which fuels itself. The harder the drug wars are fought, the more adaptive and functional become representations of drug use in terms of compulsion and helplessness as survival strategies, and so the more such a war seems to be necessary.

Drug warriors are an easy target, and much has been written about their failings and misconceptions, so we shall resist any further temptation to take yet another rhetorical swing at this group. Of more concern are the ways in which those of us who do not espouse this cause also contribute energy to the "addiction system", because we may not be aware that we are actually doing it. The key issue which proves virtually impossible to resolve concerns the clash of individual costs and benefits with societal costs and benefits. For cultural and historical reasons, the worth of the individual is highly prized in our own society. Whether we ourselves have right- or left-wing political leanings we for the most part find quite unacceptable those political regimes within which individual worth is totally subjugated to the greater service of the state, whether epitomised by Hitler's Germany, Stalin's Russia or Orwell's *1984*. In a word, therefore, we like to help individual people with their problems, whether these involve drugs, spouses, work, mortgages, health, or whatever. And this creates a problem in the specific area of addiction and drug use.

Adding fuel to the system

The problem is that where drug-related problems are concerned, the good outcome at the individual level is only achieved at the price of publicly endorsing a view of addiction which is counter-productive and which actually reinforces all those mythological beliefs about drug use which have been discussed in this and a previous book. Solving the local or individual problem in ways that are individually helpful or that "work for people" usually makes the global problem less manageable, and stores up worse problems for the future. In a word, good results are obtained from actions that reinforce misperceptions and stereotypes, ways that add fuel to mythical conceptualisations of addiction.

Consider certain types of alcohol policy currently being implemented by certain large British firms (Hutcheson, Henderson & Davies, 1995). According to many of these policies, an employee found to test positive for alcohol whilst at work would normally be subject to disciplinary procedures. However, if that person can provide evidence of a prior history of problematic alcohol use, the habit is considered a health issue, with the appropriate dispensation involving treatment and rehabilitation. This works in a humane and compassionate manner at the level of the individual with the longer term problem, who keeps a job that he/she might otherwise have lost. But again there is a price to pay. The difference between the two types of dispensation implies a pattern of drinking for which there is no individual responsibility i.e. "addicted" drinking. It is by no means clear that this distinction exists in any readily demonstrable form, or indeed, that it exists at all as a scientific phenomenon. Nonetheless, those are the "rules of the game", so in the circumstances described (i.e. negative sanctions associated with the former, and an equally clear positive payoff for the latter) there is clear advantage to be gained from explanations which are "addicted". Evidence exists (Davies *et al.*, 1997) that such a policy may actually encourage the strategic use of addicted styles of explanation in certain sections of the workforce. And as argued previously, addicted explanations for personal behaviour are actually unhelpful from a public health perspective insofar as they are associated with uncontrolled use and inability to cut down or quit.

A second example deals with another issue with which the author has had some personal involvement, and concerns expert witness testimony in courts of law. It is still highly possible for young and not-so-young people to go to prison for offences concerning possession with intent to supply cannabis, and other illicit, but "soft", drugs. Some of these drugs are in fairly widespread use across all social classes, where the harm they cause to most users appears to be minimal. It is not unreasonable therefore to hold the opinion that heavy penalties and prison sentences are not the appropriate way to deal with this problem, since few people experience harm and few people become "addicted". Where the defendant has been found in possession of, say, cannabis in quantities which are judged to be too great for personal use, the prosecution goes for a "supply" charge whilst the defence invariably centres around *how much* is appropriate for personal use in this case (since the greater this amount, the less robust becomes the evidence for the *supply* part of the charge, and it is this part of the charge which generally attracts the most punitive dispensations). In this situation therefore it is in the defendant's best interest to maximise the amount necessary for personal use and this is best done by finding evidence for heavy dependent use or "addiction". If this can be demonstrated, the defendant may well be faced with some community service and some treatment instead of the more daunting prospect of gaol. The logic is thus perfect, but semantically ridiculous. Because certain drugs appear to be relatively harmless and cause few health or "addiction" problems, the aim is to keep the accused out of gaol. This is best achieved by arguing that he/she is a helpless dependent user of the very drug in question, and is ("therefore") not in control of his/her actions. By arguing along this line, the individual may with luck be "saved" from a particularly unhelpful and nasty fate. But the out-of-touch view of drugs and their effects which is generally held by courts, court officials and juries, is re-affirmed and strengthened.

It seems likely that quite soon another example may take centre stage, in the form of litigation against tobacco companies. Smokers experiencing health problems will seek compensation in the courts, on the basis that due to the "addictive" properties of nicotine, they were unable to stop smoking. This David and Goliath scenario can only be seen as the little man or woman fighting the might of the international tobacco giants. But if the little man/woman wins, it will give credence to a view of smoking as an addiction which will actually make it less likely that others will be able to stop. Evidence reviewed in a previous chapter showed how belief that one is "addicted" is an actual barrier to attempts at quitting, and reduces the likelihood that such attempts will succeed. From a public health perspective, therefore, the "addict" label is a positive hindrance. Furthermore, the data from the study described in the last chapter also lend support to the idea that "helpless addict" (Type 3) discourse tends to accompany problematic and uncontrolled substance use.

It is suggested here that anecdotes similar to the above could be produced from virtually any sphere where alcohol and/or drug problems intersect with other spheres of activity. This would clearly include treatment agencies. The basic problem, it is suggested, is that the functionality of type 3 discourse is not confined to users themselves, but extends to many other walks of life at the point where these intersect with problems of substance use and abuse. And the problem arises because the functional "addiction" explanation works so well at the individual level; it removes responsibility, it allows others to forgive, and because of Western systems of ethics and morality it gives permission for us to take courses of action that we may not take with respect to bad things which are done *on purpose*. However, in doing so, the individual or local problem is always solved at the price of endorsing a view of substance use which at the end of the day provides further ammunition for use in the larger drug wars, and makes things worse at a more general level.

Because of the logical and moral impasse that we have created for ourselves with respect to illicit drugs, tackling local or individual problems with humanity and compassion almost always requires adding further energy to the central "addiction" concept; a concept which, it has been argued, is both philosophically flawed and empirically insupportable in a number of key respects; most notably with respect to the issues of compulsion and volition. Furthermore, it gives rise to courses of political action that actually make things worse rather than better. The principal social benefit of the "addicted" explanation within a Western system of ethics is that such an explanation justifies the forgiveness of others, and makes accessible certain other things that come with forgiveness. But that is its only advantage, and it is bought at a price. The price is that energy is added to a chain-reaction that, like an out-of-control nuclear pile, has the capacity to self-sustain and grow in energy, at an ever increasing rate.

Perhaps the greatest challenge to the addiction sciences is how to escape from this dilemma; how to cater for the needs of individual drug users who fail to manage their habits successfully, without at the same time endorsing a view of addiction which is scientifically impossible and adding fuel to social policies on drugs that turn a society against its own members for nothing more momentous than attempting to change their own individual states of consciousness. Since one might have little confidence in politicians' ability to do anything that is not immediately tied to the prospects of success at the next election, the resolution of the problem lies squarely on the shoulders of addiction researchers and theorists. It is for them to demonstrate the basic illogicality of the addiction concept, and reveal it as a functional social construction and not an objective reality. This is unlikely to happen for some time, however, given the outdated and philosophically flawed view of science with still guides much research, and which is still passed on to our unsuspecting students. At the very least we should tell them that an alternative view of "truth" is possible; then at least we may have hope for the future.

References

American Psychiatric Association (1994) *DSM IV Diagnostic and Statistical Manual of Mental Disorders*. Washington: APA.

ANASTASI, A. (1961) *Psychological Testing* (2nd ed). New York: Macmillan.

ASSITER, A & CAROL, A (1993) *Bad Girls and Dirty Pictures: The Challenge to Reclaim Feminism*. London: Pluto Press.

BALL, J.C. (1967) The reliability and validity of interview data obtained from 59 narcotic drug addicts. *American Journal of Sociology*, 72, 650–659.

BEAUCHAMP, D. (1987) Lifestyle, public health and paternalism. *In* Doxiadis, S (ed.) *Ethical Dilemmas in Health Promotion (p.72)*. Chichester: John Wiley & Sons.

BEM, D. (1972) Self-perception theory. *In* BERKOWITZ, L. (ed.) *Advances in Experimental Social Psychology*. Hillsdale: Erlbaum.

BEST, D., MORTIMER, R., MACMILLAN, D., and DAVIES, J.B. (1995) *Fast Forward Peer Research Project: Evaluation Report*. Edinburgh: Report to Fast Forward (Leith)/Scottish Office.

CAIN, R.A. (1995) Letter. *The Psychologist*. 8, 2, 56.

CAROL, A. (1994) *Nudes, Prudes and Attitudes: – Pornography and Censorship*. Cheltenham: New Clarion Press.

CARROL, L. (1896) *Alice Through the Looking Glass*. London: Beaverbrok (undated).

CHRISTO, G. (1995) *Understanding the processes of relapse and recovery: a longitudinal study of drug users in abstinence oriented treatment*. Ph.D. thesis. University of London.

COGGANS, N. & McKELLAR, S. (1994) Drug use amongst peers: peer pressure or peer preference? *Drugs: Education, Prevention and Policy,* 1, 1, 15–26, Carfax.

Concise Oxford Dictionary (1990) New York: Oxford University Press.

CONWAY, M.A. (1992) Developments and debates in the study of human memory (plus peer commentaries). *The Psychologist,* 5, 10, 439–440.

COX, T.C., JACOBS, M.R., LEBLANC, A.E. & MARSHMAN, J.A. (1983) *Drugs and Drugs Abuse.* Toronto: Addiction Research Foundation.

CRISP, Q. (1985) *The Naked Civil Servant.* London: Harper Collins Ltd.

DALLY, A. (1990) Drugspeak. *In* WARBURTON, D.M. (ed.) *Addiction Controversies.* London: Harwood Academic Press.

DAVIES, J.B. (1993) *The Myth of Addiction.* London: Harwood Academic.

DAVIES, J.B. (1996) Reasons and causes: understanding substance users explanations for their behaviour. *Human Psychopharmacology,* 11, S39–S48.

DAVIES, J.B. (1996) Health Research: Need for a methodological revolution? *Health Education Research,* 11, 2, i-iv.

DAVIES, J.B. (in press, 1997) Conversations with drug users: a functional discourse model. (The derivation of a typology of drug discourse; and an empirical study of its predictive usefulness.) *Addiction Research* 5, 1.

DAVIES, J.B. and BAKER, R. (1987) The impact of self-presentation and interviewer bias on self-reported heroin use. *British Journal of Addiction,* 82, 907-912.

DAVIES, J.B. & BEST, D.W. (1996) Demand characteristics and research into drug use. *Psychology and Health.* 11, 291–299.

DAVIES, J.B. and STACEY, B. (1972) *Teenagers and Alcohol,* London: HMSO.

DAVIES, J.B., WRIGHT, L.B., (1997) HUTCHESON, G.D., HENDERSON, M.M., HEPBURN, A., McPHERSON, A and FOX, A. *Alcohol in the Workplace: results of an Empirical Study.* London: Department of Education and employment (in press).

DEWEY, J. (1933) *How We Think.* New York: Heath.

DiCLEMENTE, C.C. and PROCHASKA, J.O. (1985) Processes and stages of self-change: coping and competence is smoking behaviour change. *In* SHIFFMAN, S. and WILLS, T.A. (eds.) *Coping and Substance Use.* (ch. 13) New York: Academic Press.

EDWARDS, D. & POTTER, J. (1992) *Discursive Psychology.* London: Sage.

EDWARDS, D. POTTER, J. and MIDDLETON, D. (1992) Toward a discursive psychology of remembering (plus peer commentaries) *The Psychologist* 5, 10, 441–446.

EDWARDS, G., BABOR, T.F., RAW, M. & STOCKWELL, T. Playing fair; science, ethics and scientific journals. *Addiction* 1995, 90, pp 3-8.

EISER, R., and GOSSOP, M.R. (1979) "Hooked" or "sick"; addicts' perceptions of their addiction. *Addictive Behaviours* 4, 185-191.

EISER, J., and van der PLIGT (1986) Smoking cessation and smokers perceptions of their addiction. *Journal of Social and Clinical Psychology* 4, 1, 60-70.

EISER, J.R., van der PLIGT, J., RAW, M. and SUTTON, S.R. (1985). Trying to stop smoking: effects of perceived addiction, attributions for failure, and expectancy of success. *Journal of Behavioural Medicine* 8, 4, 321-341.

EVANS, C. (1978) *Psychology: A Dictionary of the Mind, Brain and Behaviour.* London: Hutchison Publishing.

FISHBEIN, M., and AJZEN, I. (1975) *Belief, Attitude, Intention and Behaviour: an Introduction to Theory and Research.* Boston: Addison-Wesley.

FRIEDMAN, M. & SZASZ, T.S. (1992) *On Liberty and Drugs.* Washington: Drug Policy Foundation.

FRISCHER, M. (1994) *Multi-city study of Drug Misuse: First Glasgow Report* (Pompidou Group), Glasgow: Ruchill Hospital.

GOSSOP, M., EISER, R., and WARD, E. (1982) The addict's perception of their own drug taking: implications for the treatment of drug dependence. *Addictive Behaviours,* 7, 189-194.

GREEN, D.M. & SWETS, J.A. (1966) *Signal Detection Theory and Psychophysics.* New York: John Wiley & Sons Inc.

GROVE, J.R. (1993) Attributional correlates of cessation self-efficacy among smokers. *Addictive Behaviours,* 18, 311-320.

HARRISON, L. and MUGFORD, S. (1994) eds. Cocaine in the Community. *Addiction Research,* 2; 1.

HIGGINS, E.T. and BARGH, J.A. (1987) Social cognition and social perception. *Annual Review of Psychology,* 38, 369-425.

HUTCHESON, G.D., HENDERSON, M.M. and DAVIES, J.B. (1995) *Alcohol in the Workplace: Costs and Responses.* London: Department for Education and Employment.

JENKS, R.J. (1994) Attitudes and perceptions towards smoking. Smokers' views of themselves and other smokers. *Journal of Social Psychology,* 134, 3, 355–361.

JESSOR, R., GRAVES, T.D., HANSON, R.C. and JESSOR, S.L.

(1968) *Society, Personality and Deviant Behaviour.* New York: Holt, Rinehart and Winston.

KATZ, D. (1960) The functional approach to the study of attitudes. *Public Opinion Quarterly.* 24, 163-204.

KATZ, R.C. and SINGH, N.N. (1985) Reflections on the ex-smoker: some findings on successful quitters. *Journal of Behavioural Medicine,* 9, 2, 191–202.

KOCH, S. (1964) Psychology and emerging conceptions of knowledge as unitary. In Wann, T.W. (ed) *Behaviourism and Phenomenology.* Chicago: University of Chicago Press.

KOESTLER, A. (1964) *The Act of Creation.* London: Hutchinson & Co. (Ch 1 and 2).

LAWSON, H. APPIGNANESI, L. (1989) *Dismantling Truth.* London: Weidenfeld & Nicolson.

LYON, J. (1995) Letter. *The Psychologist.* 8, 4, 154.

MARSH, P. ROSSER, E. & HARRE, R. (1978) *The Rules of Disorder.* London: Routledge and Kegan Paul.

MAYNARD, M. (1990) The re-shaping of sociology? Trends in the study of gender. *Sociology,* 24920; 269-90.

MEAD, G.H. (1932) *The Philosophy of the Present.* Chicago: Open Court.

McALLISTER, P. & DAVIES, J.B. (1992) Attributional bias as a function of clinical classification. *Drug Issues,* 22, 5.

McKEGANEY, N. (1995) Quantitative and qualitative research in the addictions: an unhelpful divide. *Addiction.* 90, 749-751.

McMURRAN, M. (1994) *The Psychology of Addiction.* London: Taylor and Francis.

McNICOL, D. (1972) *A Primer of Signal Detection Theory.* Sydney: Allen and Unwin.

MILES, M.B. & HUBERMAN, M.A. (1984) *Qualitative Data Analysis: A Sourcebook of New Methods.* London: Sage.

NISBET, R.E. & WILSON, T.D. (1977) Telling more than we can know: verbal reports on mental processes. *Psychological Review,* 84, 3, 231-259.

PLANT, M.A. and MILLER, T.I. (1977) Disguised and undisguised questionnaire compared: two alternative approaches to drinking behaviour surveys. *Social Psychiatry,* 12, 21-24.

POPPER, K. (1959) *The Logic of Scientific Discovery.* Hutchinson: London.

PROCHASKA, J.O. and DiCLEMENTI, C.C. (1982) Transtheoretical therapy: toward a more integrated model of change. *Psychotherapy: Theory Research and Practice,* 19, 276-288.

PROCHASKA, J.O. and DiCLEMENTE C.C. (1986) Toward a comprehensive model of change. *In* MILLER, W. and HEATHER, N. (eds). *Treating Addictive Behaviours.* New York: Plenum.

ROSENTHAL, R. (1966) *Experimenter Effects in Behavioural Research.* New York: Appleton Century Crofts.

SAUNDERS, B. (1995) Illicit Drugs and Harm Reduction Education (editorial) *Addiction Research,* 2, 4, i-iii.

SCHARF, B. (1975) *Experimental Sensory Psychology,* Illinois: Scott, Foresman & Co.

SHEWAN, D., DAVIES, J.B. & HENDERSON, M. (1992) *Drug use and HIV/AIDS in Prisons in Scotland, France, Italy and Spain.* Public Health Unit of the Commission of European Communities.

SHIBLI, S. (1992) Personal communication. Unpublished data from Ph.D. thesis, in progress. University of Strathclyde, Glasgow.

SHUTE, R. (1995) Letter. *The Psychologist.* 8, 2, 155.

SILVERMAN, D. (1985) *Qualitative Methodology and Sociology.* Hampshire: Gower Publishing.

SIMPSON, J. (1994) *This Game of Ghosts.* Vintage Books. London: Random House.

SKINNER, B.F. (1938) *The Behaviour of Organisms: an Experimental Analysis.* New York: Appleton-Century Crofts.

SKINNER, B.F. (1948) *Walden Two.* New York: Macmillan.

SKINNER, B.F. (1953) *Science and Human Behaviour.* New York: Macmillan.

SKINNER, B.F. (1957) *Verbal Behaviour.* New York: Appleton Century Crofts.

SKINNER, B.F. (1974) *About Behaviourism.* London: Jonathan Cape.

SKINNER, B.F. (1978) *Reflection on Behaviorism and Society.* New Jersey: Prentice-Hall.

Surgeon General (1988) *Nicotine Addiction: The Health Consequences of Smoking.* Maryland: US Department of Health and Human Services.

WARD, J., MATTICK, R., and HALL, W. (1992) *Key Issues in Methadone Maintenance Treatment.* New South Wales University Press.

Index